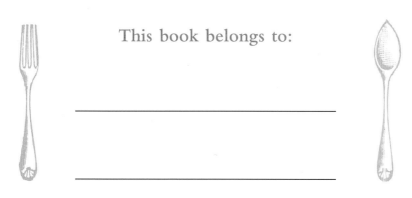

This book belongs to:

_____

_____

Rose Marie Donhauser

Lemons & Oranges

Favorite Recipes

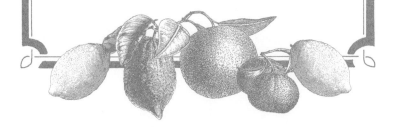

Design: Niels Bonnemeier
Production: Patty Holden
Translator: Christie Tam
Editors: Monika Römer, Randy Mann, Lisa M. Tooker
Published originally under the title Zitronen & Orangen
©2003 Verlag W. Hölker GmbH, Münster
English translation for the U.S. market ©2004 Silverback Books, Inc.

ISBN: 1-930603-98-3

Printed in China

CONTENTS

Unless otherwise indicated, all recipes make four servings.

PREFACE

Can you imagine summer without fresh-squeezed lemonade or salmon served without lemon wedges. Many of us would find it hard to serve and eat our favorite drinks and dishes if fresh lemons and limes were not readily available at local supermarkets or grown right in our own garden.

My love of lemons and limes has mainly come from my steadily growing collection of recipes that use citrus fruits, which I've been developing and writing down for a number of years. Often it's no more than a drop of juice or a trace of citrus fruit aroma—but without it, the recipes would only be half as good or no good at all!

Citrus fruits have been in constant use for many years because they're the true jacks of all trades. In home kitchens, lemon and lime juice are the perfect "fragrance" for fried fish and grilled lamb. In restaurants and ice cream shops, oranges, lemons, and limes are stacked up high awaiting their processing into creams, sorbets, and countless ice cream flavors. In bakeries, candied orange and lemon peel are kept in abundance for use in various cakes and tortes. And in bars, drinks are thoroughly shaken with lime or grapefruit juice and then garnished with citrus slices and sugared rims. Citrus fruits are used and loved everywhere, from cold dishes to hot, as well as behind the bar.

But if you take a closer look, you'll see that oranges, mandarin oranges, lemons, limes, and grapefruits are much more commonly enjoyed raw than they are processed for foods and drinks. The miracle ingredient behind this phenomenon is vitamin C! Whenever the cold and flu season approaches, the consumption of fresh-squeezed juices soars. But the same is true in summer when high temperatures increase the demand for the aroma of the more sour members of the citrus family, namely lemons and limes. Nevertheless, this cookbook is mainly concerned with the simpler as well as more elaborate processing of fruits in cuisine.

Oranges and lemons can be prepared in so many different ways and provide so much material worth knowing and telling, that I could easily have filled the pages of one cookbook for each fruit. But often it comes down to the right combination. Nor should we forget the citrus cousins, which provide enjoyable reading and even more enjoyable cooking.

And so, to put you in the right mood for cooking and eating, I recommend a fancy meal based on this very book: As an opening cocktail, serve Lime Caipirinha. As the appetizer, try Vitello Tonatto with Lemon Wedges, followed by an entrée of Red Mullet on Mandarin-Orange Wild Rice and a dessert of Crêpes Suzette with Oranges. And just so the grapefruit won't feel left out, offer the Fruity Fitness Crudités for munching in between.

So, bon appetit with these fresh tastes that will add sweetness and zest to your life.

THE MANY BRANCHES OF
THE CITRUS FAMILY TREE

Citrus plants, which include over 60 species belonging to the rutaceae family, are natives of Asia, and particularly of Southeast, East, and South Asia. Over the years, however, new cultivated varieties have been popping up constantly and hybrids are being cultivated in almost all tropical and subtropical countries. Botanically speaking, citrus plants are classified as berry fruit. The most important examples are the orange, mandarin orange, satsuma, tangerine, lemon, lime, and grapefruit.

Lemons—Sweet and Sour Vitamin Bursts

The light- to golden-yellow lemon (*Citrus limon*) with its rough peel of varying thickness grows on trees 10- to 20-feet high. The lemon is the most important member of the citrus family. This can be attributed to its versatility in both culinary and health applications as well as in cosmetics, all of which is based on its nutritional values: 100 grams of raw fruit contain 36 calories, 0.8 g protein, 0.6 g fat, 3.2 g available carbohydrates, and 4.4 g fiber. They provide 54 mg of vitamin C with trace amounts of vitamins B and A, and also contain minerals such as calcium, phosphorus, sodium and, most importantly, 28 mg magnesium and 144 mg potassium.

Fresh lemons can be found in virtually every household or, at the very least, lemon juice in serving-size containers, small plastic lemons, small bottles, or large bottles. There is always a need for lemon juice, whether as a shot of seasoning in sauces or dishes, for drizzling on fish or meat, for flavoring tea, as a mandatory ingredient in cocktails, as an acidifier and a preservative, or as an aid to digestion with fatty dishes. Often it's the lemon that adds just the right zing, for that trace of extravagance and, of course, that wonderfully fragrant freshness.

Throughout history, lemon juice has been highly valued both for its unique flavoring capacity and in the treatment of illness. In her cookbooks, Hildegard von Bingen wrote that lemon juice helps fight fever. The ancient Romans used lemon juice as an antidote to poison and a cure for gout. And that culinary genius and ladies' man Giacomo Girolamo Casanova (1725–1798) discovered that lemon juice could be used as a contraceptive.

And, finally, the latest nutritional findings indicate that lemon juice is a "magic potion" that can be rubbed onto cellulite and, if we can believe the advertisements, even dissolve it. In any case, citric acid does boost your metabolism and, as a carrier of vitamin C, performs important functions in your body in its capacity as the "health police."

Limes—the Lemon's Green Little Sister

The egg-sized, thin-peeled, yellow- to light-green lime (*Citrus aurantifolia*) grows on a small tree or tree-like bush. Its flesh is much juicier than that of the lemon and just a touch more tart. We've mainly come to know this little fruit through the growing popularity of the Caipirinha cocktail, but also as a flavoring in innumerable spicy curry dishes from Asia. The species we call lime came from East Asia and is cultivated all year round in orchards in Mexico, Egypt, and California. Nowhere is the Margarita as popular as here, and Mexican cuisine has helped the lime graduate to new levels of appeal.

Regardless of which of the two varieties you use, you can almost always substitute lemon juice in a recipe calling for lime juice. But you should then increase the amount of juice slightly to obtain a comparable strength.

The kaffir lime (*Citrus hystrix*), like the conventional lime, grows on a small tree or tree-like bush but has a bumpy green rind. It originally came from Thailand but is now cultivated in Central America and Africa. Although kaffir limes are not very juicy, the juice and peel (especially when grated) are extremely aromatic. And more importantly, Thai cooking would probably cease to be Thai without the leaves, which are not eaten, but add unforgettable flavor.

Grapefruits—Originally Imported from Malaysia

There is some confusion in the terminology used for the grapefruit (*Citrus paradisi*). It is also called a pamplemousse—although this actually refers to an entirely different fruit, the pomelo. The confusion is compounded by the fact that the two names are used synonymously in many European languages, and in some languages both these fruits are called by a single name.

The first of the two to come on the scene was the pomelo (*Citrus grandis* or *Citrus maxima*), also known as a pummelo, Chinese grapefruit or shaddock. It is the largest and heaviest member of the citrus family, reaching diameters of up to 10 inches and weighing about 13 pounds. These yellow, thick-peeled fruits play a subordinate role on the market, mainly due to their fibrous and bitter segments that are difficult to detach. The grapefruit is probably an accidental West-Indian hybrid between the pomelo and orange. Its name comes from the belief that grapefruits grew in clusters like grapes. In fact, they grow individually on trees 26- to 49-feet high. Grapefruits are cultivated everywhere that citrus fruits grow, the main regions being the U.S., South Africa, Israel, and Italy, where they are harvested all year round.

Depending on the type, grapefruits can have a light-yellow to pink rind. Their whitish-green to yellow flesh tastes sour to bitter. The rule of thumb is that grapefruits with yellow flesh are sourer and bitterer than those with pink flesh. An Israeli variety with a yellow to green rind has recently appeared on the market. Its flesh tastes sweeter than that of other grapefruits and is therefore very appropriately named the "Sweetie."

In the diet industry, grapefruits are especially valued, not only because of their low calorie content, but also due to the fact that the flesh promotes digestion, has a purging effect, and speeds up the metabolism. Generally speaking, grapefruits are seldom used in cooking. Rather, they are almost always eaten raw—cut in half crosswise and sprinkled with sugar.

Oranges—Embassadors from Asia

The orange tree (*Citrus sinensis*) is a native of China and grows up to 33-feet high. In about the 11th century, the Arabs brought the orange tree to Southern Europe. Our name "orange" was derived from the Persian word "narang," which basically means "bitter." The first oranges actually were bitter and their taste was improved only by cultivation.

Oranges are available all year round. A distinction is made between winter oranges, imported from November to June from Italy, Spain, Morocco and Israel, and summer oranges that arrive from June to November from the U.S., South Africa, and South America.

Oranges fall into three main categories, encompassing all the individual varieties: Yellow-orange oranges with yellow-orange flesh, semi-blood oranges with red flesh but a yellow-orange peel, and blood oranges whose peel and flesh are both red.

Favorites in Europe are the thin-peeled variety with few seeds from Italy, oranges from Jaffa in Israel with a somewhat thicker peel, and the seedless navel oranges from Morocco and Spain. The moro orange, an especially tasty variety of blood orange, is imported in January from Sicily but, unfortunately, has only a very short season.

Mandarin Oranges, Satsumas, and Tangerines— Pure Aroma

The mandarin orange (*Citrus reticulat*) is the fruit of a tree 20- to 26-feet high that originally came from the island of Mauritius. It carries the name of the island, as it's called by its inhabitants. Today, "mandarin" is a general term applied to a number of species, varieties, and hybrids that are cultivated in Asia, America, and the entire Mediterranean region. Here are some of the most important: We know the Japanese mandarin under the name "satsuma." It has a loose, smooth peel and pale orange flesh. Some botanists also classify the tangerine, originally from Southeast Asia, as a separate type of mandarin orange. It is small and aromatic but contains a lot of seeds. The clementine orange, a favorite seedless variety, actually is not a mandarin orange at all, but a cross between the mandarin and Seville orange. Today, over 100 different varieties of mandarin orange are recognized worldwide, and we can expect even more new types in the future.

Kumquats, Ugli Fruit, and Citrons—
Lesser Known Family Members

To complete our portrait of the citrus family, let's look at three other members that also have their place on the market:

The kumquat (*Fortunella japonica*) originated in China. This small, oval fruit grows on thorny bushes and is similar to an orange but in a miniature format. It has a thin, sweet peel and juicy, slightly bitter flesh, and is generally eaten fresh with the peel still on. However, you can also cook and use kumquats to make marmalade, jelly, and syrup.

The ugli fruit from Jamaica is a relatively well-known hybrid between the tangerine and grapefruit (*Citrus tangerina*, *Citrus paradisi*, and *Citrus sinesis*). It has a rough, thick peel and a surprisingly sweet, juicy, aromatic flesh.

Finally, there is the citron (*Citrus medica*). Unlike other citrus fruits, it is cultivated not for its flesh but for its thick, fragrant rind. A citron can weigh at least six pounds and grow up to 10-inches long. The very thick, green-to-yellow, rough, and warty peel of the unripe fruit provides us with the popular candied orange peel, produced by preserving the peel in a sugar solution. This "giant lemon" is grown in tropical and subtropical regions, but primarily in orchards near the Mediterranean region where it is harvested year round.

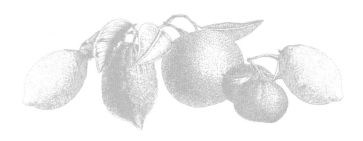

SOUPS AND APPETIZERS

Carrot Orange Soup

1 onion, 2 cloves garlic, ¾-inch piece fresh ginger root, 1 lb carrots,
1 large potato, ¼ cup olive oil, Salt, Freshly ground black pepper,
3 cups vegetable stock, 2 oranges, ¾ cup heavy cream,
2 tbs mango chutney (prepared product), 1–2 tbs chopped parsley

Peel onion, garlic, ginger, carrots and potato, and dice finely. In a saucepan, heat oil and braise prepared vegetables for 2 minutes while stirring. Season with salt and pepper and pour in stock. Bring to a boil and then simmer vegetables over medium heat for about 20 minutes.

In the meantime, squeeze juice from 1 orange. Peel the other orange so that the white outer membrane is also removed and cut segments from between the inner membranes, saving any juice that escapes. Use a hand blender to purée the soup and enrich with cream and mango chutney. Add seasoning to taste. Distribute orange segments in small soup bowls or cups. Pour soup on top, drizzle with orange juice, and sprinkle with parsley.

Goes with slices of hearty, fresh farmer's bread, preferably spread with a little wild garlic pesto.

Yogurt Cucumber Soup with Salmon and Oranges

4 stalks dill, 1 large cucumber, 1¼ cups plain yogurt, Salt,
Freshly ground black pepper, 1 pinch cayenne pepper,
½ tsp crushed coriander seeds, 2 oranges,
10 oz fresh skinless salmon fillet, Juice of ½ lemon,
1 tsp Worcestershire sauce, 1 tbs butter

Rinse dill, pluck leaves from stalks, and chop finely. Peel cucumber and cut into small pieces. In a bowl, combine cucumber and yogurt and purée finely with a hand blender. Season with salt, pepper, cayenne, and coriander.

Peel orange so that the white outer membrane is also removed and cut segments from between the inner membranes. Cut salmon into uniform strips and mix with lemon juice and Worcestershire sauce. In a pan, heat butter and sauté salmon strips on all sides for 4–5 minutes. Season with salt and pepper.

Pour cucumber soup into soup plates and arrange salmon strips in the center of each plate. Decoratively arrange orange segments around the edges and sprinkle soup with chopped dill.

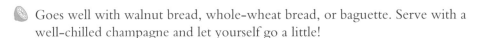 Goes well with walnut bread, whole-wheat bread, or baguette. Serve with a well-chilled champagne and let yourself go a little!

Thai Shrimp Soup

You will find the ingredients for this national soup of Thailand in any well-stocked Asian or specialty Thai store.

2 cloves garlic, 2 stalks lemon grass, 2 shallots, 4 small chile peppers,
5 oz oyster mushrooms, 10 oz peeled shrimp, 4½ cups chicken stock,
4 kaffir lime leaves, 2–3 tbs Thai fish sauce, 1 tsp chili paste in oil,
Juice of 1 lime, 1 tbs chopped cilantro

Peel garlic. Clean lemon grass and cut up coarsely. Crush garlic and lemon grass with the back of a knife blade. Peel shallots and cut into strips. Remove stems from chile peppers. Clean oyster mushrooms and cut into strips. Rinse shrimp, slit open down the back, and remove veins.

In a saucepan or wok, heat chicken stock and stir in prepared ingredients. Season with kaffir lime leaves, fish sauce, chili paste, and lime juice. As soon as soup starts to boil, reduce heat, add shrimp, and cook gently for 5–8 minutes. Pour into preheated bowls and sprinkle with cilantro.

 Before serving, you can remove the garlic, chile peppers, lime leaves, and lemon grass, which function simply as flavor enhancers. In Thailand and Thai restaurants, however, they are served in the soup.

Greek Lemon Soup with Chicken

1 stewing chicken (about 2 lb), Salt,
1 bunch soup greens (e.g., carrot, celery stalk with leaves,
celery root, parsnip, fennel bulb, leek, onion, parsley),
2 bay leaves, 2 eggs, Juice of 2 lemons, Freshly ground black pepper

Rinse chicken thoroughly under cold running water, place in a pot, and add enough cold water to cover chicken. Add salt, bring to a boil, and skim off any foam that forms on the surface with a skimmer.

In the meantime, clean soup greens and cut up coarsely. Rinse parsley, pat dry, pluck off leaves, chop finely, and set aside. Add remaining soup greens and bay leaves to the pot. Cook over medium heat for about 1 hour until the flesh detaches easily from the bones. Remove chicken from stock, let cool briefly, then remove skin, debone, and cut meat into bite-sized pieces.

Pour soup through a strainer, return to a boil, and remove from heat. Place a ladleful of soup in a bowl and whisk together with eggs. Slowly stir in lemon juice and then stir this mixture into the soup when it is no longer boiling. Add chicken meat and parsley and season to taste with salt and pepper.

 You can also make this soup in the Greek style by cooking ½ cup rice in the soup. Kali orexi (bon appetit)!

Gorgonzola Spinach with Oranges

1 lb fresh spinach, Salt, 1 onion, 2 cloves garlic,
6–7 oz Gorgonzola cheese, 2½ oranges, 3 tbs butter,
½ cup herb crème fraîche, Freshly ground black pepper,
⅓ cup pine nuts, Lemon pepper (optional)

Clean spinach, rinse, and blanch in boiling, salted water for 1 minute. Pour into a colander, rinse under cold water, and drain. Squeeze out excess liquid with your hands and chop a little smaller.

Peel and mince onion and garlic. Cut Gorgonzola into small pieces. Peel 2 oranges so that the white outer membrane is also removed and cut segments from between the inner membranes. Squeeze juice from remaining orange half.

In a large pan, heat butter and briefly braise onion and garlic. Stir in herb crème fraîche. Fold in spinach and Gorgonzola. Season with salt, pepper, and a little orange juice. Transfer spinach to 4 preheated plates and arrange orange segments on top. Garnish with pine nuts and lemon pepper.

 This delicious spinach not only makes a good appetizer but is also a real treat when served as a separate dish for vegetarians. It can also be a side dish with, for example, grilled fish.

Sauerkraut with Mandarin Oranges

1 onion, 5 mandarin oranges, $\frac{1}{4}$ cup vegetable oil,
16 oz sauerkraut (canned), $\frac{1}{2}$ cup meat stock, Salt,
1 pinch sugar, 1 tbs freshly chopped parsley

Peel and mince onion. Squeeze juice from 3 mandarin oranges. Peel the other 2, separate the segments, and set aside. In a wide pot, heat vegetable oil and briefly braise onion. Pull apart sauerkraut with a fork and stir in. Pour in meat stock and mandarin orange juice and as soon as it starts to boil, reduce to low heat, and simmer gently for 15 minutes. Season with salt and sugar. Just before serving, add parsley and mandarin orange segments.

 Serve this fancy sauerkraut creation as an appetizer with crispy bacon strips, as a side dish with grilled smoked pork sausage, or alone as a low-calorie dish.

Fruit Canapés with Ham and Parmesan

1 papaya, 1 orange, 2 mandarin oranges, 1 grapefruit,
5 oz thinly sliced, cooked ham, 5 oz Parma ham,
5 oz dried beef (cut paper thin),
1$\frac{1}{2}$ cups freshly grated Parmesan cheese (loosely packed)
Plus: Toothpicks

Peel all fruits. Remove seeds from papaya and remove white membrane from citrus fruits. Cut peeled fruits into bite-sized, uniform pieces. Cut all types of ham into suitably sized pieces, wrap around the fruit, and secure with toothpicks. Decoratively arrange on 4 plates or 1 large platter and sprinkle with Parmesan.

 Serve with tortilla chips and salsa or walnut bread with wild garlic pesto. These fruit canapés are the ideal accompaniment to Prosecco, sparkling wine, or champagne.

Orange Asparagus on Cooked Ham

2 lb asparagus, Salt, 1 pinch sugar, 1 dash lemon juice, 1 tsp butter
For the sauce: 5 oranges, 1 tbs sherry vinegar, 1 egg yolk,
½ cup olive oil, Salt, Freshly ground black pepper,
1 tbs orange liqueur (e.g., Grand Marnier)
Plus: 6 oz shaved, cooked ham, 1 tbs chopped parsley

Clean asparagus. In a saucepan, combine water, salt, sugar, lemon juice, and butter, add asparagus and cook for about 15 minutes until al dente, then remove.

In the meantime, make the sauce: Rinse 1 orange under hot water and wipe dry with a cloth. Grate off peel and set aside. Squeeze juice from all oranges and pour juice through a fine-mesh strainer. Using an electric hand mixer, vigorously beat orange juice and remaining sauce ingredients. Place asparagus spears in a casserole dish, pour sauce over the top, and marinate at room temperature for 1 hour.

Spread ham slices over the surface of 4 appetizer plates or a large platter, and distribute orange asparagus on top. Garnish with grated orange peel and parsley.

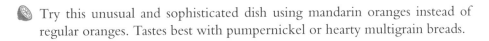 Try this unusual and sophisticated dish using mandarin oranges instead of regular oranges. Tastes best with pumpernickel or hearty multigrain breads.

Duck with Figs in Port Wine

8 oz Barbary duck breast (about ½ lb), Salt,
Freshly cracked black pepper, 2 tbs vegetable oil, 3 fresh figs,
⅓ cup port wine, 2 tbs orange marmalade
Plus: 12 oriental porcelain spoons, Fresh orange zest

Leaving on the skin, cut duck breast into 12 equal, bite-sized pieces. Season with salt and pepper. In a pan, heat vegetable oil and sauté duck pieces on all sides for 2–3 minutes until crispy. Transfer to a plate and set aside, reserving pan drippings.

Rinse figs, pat dry with paper towels, and cut into quarters. Place in the pan residues and stir for 1 minute. Add port wine and stir in orange marmalade. Add any juice that accumulates from the duck pieces.

Arrange 1 fig quarter and 1 piece of duck on each spoon and drizzle with sauce. Garnish with orange zest and place 3 spoons on each of 4 appetizer plates.

Or use 1 large appetizer platter and set the spoons out on a salad buffet.

Vitello Tonnato

*1½ lb veal from the leg, 1 bottle dry white wine, Salt,
1 dash white wine vinegar, 5 black peppercorns,
2 bay leaves, 2 whole cloves,
Small bunch soup greens (e.g., celery, parsley, leek, onion), 1 lemon
For the tuna sauce: 1 small can tuna packed in water, 4 anchovy fillets,
Juice of 1 lemon, 2 egg yolks, ⅔ cup olive oil, Salt,
Freshly ground pepper, 2 tbs capers, plus 1 tbs liquid from the jar
Plus: 2 lemons, 2 tbs capers*

The day before cooking, rinse veal under cold running water and bind it with kitchen string tightly enough so it will retain its shape when processed. Place in a bowl and add white wine and enough cold water to completely cover the meat. Cover bowl with plastic wrap and refrigerate for 1 day.

On the next day, transfer meat to a pot, pour in marinating liquid, and add 4½ cups cold water. Stir in a large pinch of salt, white wine vinegar, peppercorns, bay leaves and cloves, and bring to a boil. In the meantime, clean and chop soup greens. Rinse lemon, cut into quarters, and add lemon and soup greens to the pot. Simmer contents of the pot over medium heat for 40–45 minutes. Then remove from heat and let meat cool in the liquid.

In the meantime, make the tuna sauce: Drain tuna and rinse anchovy fillets. Combine tuna, anchovies, lemon juice, and a ladleful of veal liquid in a blender and purée. Using an electric hand mixer set to the highest speed, beat egg yolks until creamy, adding olive oil 1 teaspoonful at a time to form a thick and creamy mayonnaise. Combine tuna purée and mayonnaise and season with salt and pepper. Crush capers and add capers and caper liquid.

When veal is completely cooled, remove from the pot, drain, remove the kitchen string, and cut into very thin slices. Spread veal slices over the surface of 4 plates and spoon tuna sauce over the top. Peel lemons so that the white outer membrane is also removed and cut into slices. Distribute lemon slices and capers on the meat.

 Serve with Tuscan bread and white wine.

Lemony Tuna Sandwich

Makes 2 servings
1 lemon, 1 can tuna packed in oil, 1 tsp Worcestershire sauce,
2 tbs mayonnaise, Salt, Freshly ground black pepper,
4 leaves butterhead lettuce, 4 large slices white bread, 1 cup watercress
For the dip: 1 cup sour cream, 1 tsp tomato paste,
1 tbs chopped cilantro, 1 pinch cayenne pepper

Peel lemon so that the white outer membrane is also removed and dice fruit finely. Drain tuna thoroughly in a strainer, transfer to a bowl, and flake with a fork. Add Worcestershire sauce, mayonnaise and diced lemon, and stir to form a creamy mixture. Season with salt and pepper. Rinse lettuce leaves and cut into fine strips. Toast bread and spread 2 slices with half the tuna mixture. Scatter lettuce strips on top. Trim cress stems, rinse, pat dry, and distribute on sandwiches. Spread remaining tuna mixture on the other bread slices and press them onto the top of the sandwiches with the spread side down. Cut in half diagonally. For the dip, combine sour cream, tomato paste, cilantro and cayenne, and serve in 2 small bowls.

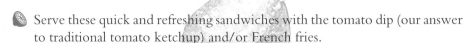 Serve these quick and refreshing sandwiches with the tomato dip (our answer to traditional tomato ketchup) and/or French fries.

Salmon with Lime Curry Dressing

2 limes, 1 lb skinless smoked salmon fillet, 4 stalks cilantro,
½ cup vegetable oil, 1 tbs curry powder, 1 tbs sesame oil,
Salt, Freshly ground black pepper

Squeeze juice from limes. Cut salmon fillets into very thin slices. Rinse cilantro, pat dry, pluck leaves from stalks, and chop finely.

In a saucepan, heat vegetable oil and brown curry lightly while stirring constantly. Add lime juice and 3 tbs water. Transfer curry sauce to a bowl to cool and season with sesame oil, salt, and pepper. Spread salmon over the surface of several large platters, drizzle with curry sauce, and sprinkle with cilantro.

 For garnish, peel 1 apple, core, cut into matchsticks, mix with 1 tbs balsamic vinegar, and pile in the center of the platter. Best served with a crusty baguette.

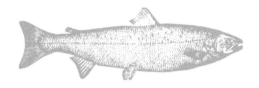

Salmon Tartar Seasoned with Caipirinha

1 lb fresh, skinless salmon fillet, 1 tbs vegetable oil, Salt,
Freshly cracked black pepper, 2 limes,
2 tsp Cachaça (sugarcane brandy), 1 tbs brown sugar
Plus: Crushed ice, 4 stalks lemon balm

Cut salmon fillet into small pieces and then chop very finely. Combine salmon and oil and season with salt and pepper. Rinse limes under hot water and wipe dry. Cut up 1 lime coarsely with the peel, place in the bottom of a tall glass, and vigorously crush and squeeze with a wooden spoon. Add Cachaça and sugar and continue processing. Strain liquid through a fine-mesh strainer and stir lightly into the chopped salmon. Distribute salmon tartar in individual bowls and arrange on top of large bowls filled with crushed ice.

Peel the second lime so that the white outer membrane is also removed and cut segments from between the inner membranes. Rinse lemon balm, pat dry, and pluck leaves from stalks. Decoratively garnish salmon servings with lime segments and lemon balm.

 Serve baked potatoes with crème fraîche, a green salad, and a well-chilled white wine (e.g., Chablis, Chardonnay). Or enjoy it with a Caipirinha.

Creamy Sole and Shrimp Terrine with Grapefruit

Makes 1 loaf pan (2 qt volume)
1 grapefruit, ½ lb peeled shrimp (about 8 oz),
½ lb sole fillets (about 8 oz), Salt, Freshly ground black pepper,
¾ cup dry white wine, ½ bunch Italian parsley, 2½ cups plain yogurt,
½ cup crème fraîche, 3 pkg powdered gelatin

Peel grapefruit so that the white outer membrane is also removed and cut segments from between the inner membranes. Squeeze remaining juice from membranes. Rinse shrimp and sole fillets, pat dry with paper towels, and flavor with grapefruit juice. Season with salt and pepper.

Bring wine to a boil, add shrimp and fish fillets, and cook gently over medium heat for 1 minute. Use a skimmer to transfer to a plate.

Let wine cool briefly, then refrigerate until it cools completely. Rinse parsley, pat dry, pluck leaves from stems, and chop finely. Line a loaf pan with plastic wrap so that it extends far beyond the ends. Combine yogurt, crème fraîche, and parsley. Season with salt and pepper. Stir powdered gelatin into cold wine until it has dissolved. Return wine to a boil, pour through a fine-mesh strainer, and let cool slightly.

Beat lukewarm wine into yogurt cream and pour a little of the mixture into the bottom of the loaf pan. Place layers of shrimp, fish fillets, and grapefruit wedges in the pan, covering each layer with a layer of yogurt cream. Finally, fold over the overhanging plastic wrap and refrigerate the pan for at least 4 hours.

To serve, turn out the terrine from the pan and remove plastic wrap. With a sharp knife, cut into slices ⅛- to ½-inch thick.

 Goes with a mâche salad with bacon croutons and oven-fresh white bread.

Citrus-Marinated Fish Fillets

1½ lb fish fillets (e.g. cod, redfish, sole), Juice of 1 lime, Salt,
2 onions, 2 carrots, 2 green bell peppers, 1 red chile pepper,
1 pink grapefruit, ½ cup olive oil, 1 tsp brown sugar,
1 large pinch each of chili powder, cayenne pepper, and cardamom,
1 tsp crushed black peppercorns, 2 bay leaves,
3−4 tbs white wine vinegar, 2 oranges

Rinse fish fillets under cold running water and pat dry. Drizzle with lime juice and salt lightly.

Peel onions and carrots and cut into fine strips. Cut bell and chile peppers in half and remove stems, seeds, and interiors. Cut bell pepper into uniform thin strips and finely dice chile pepper. Peel grapefruit so that the white outer membrane is also removed and cut segments from between the inner membranes.

In a pan, heat half the olive oil and braise vegetable strips and chile pepper with sugar for about 10 minutes. Season with chili powder, cayenne, cardamom, peppercorns, and bay leaves. Add a little cold water, pour on white wine vinegar, and gently simmer contents of the pan for another 5 minutes.

In a pan, heat remaining olive oil, sauté fish fillets on both sides for 3−4 minutes, and remove. In a shallow mold, arrange alternating layers of fish fillets, grapefruit segments, and vegetable strips, finishing with a layer of vegetables. Cover dish with plastic wrap and refrigerate for about 2 hours.

Just before serving, peel oranges so that the white outer membrane is also removed and cut segments from between the inner membranes. Decoratively arrange fish and vegetables on 4 plates and garnish with orange segments.

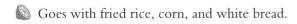 Goes with fried rice, corn, and white bread.

Crawfish on Orange Lemon Grass Sauce

2 green onions, 3 stalks lemon grass, 2 oranges, 1 mango,
½ lb fresh peeled crawfish meat (about 8 oz), Juice of ½ lime,
Salt, Freshly ground black pepper, 1 tbs butter,
1 pinch sugar, Fresh lemon balm leaves

Clean green onions and dice finely. Clean lemon grass and cut into smaller pieces. Squeeze juice from oranges. Peel mango and chop coarsely. Drizzle crawfish meat with lime juice and season with salt and pepper.

In a small saucepan, heat butter and briefly braise green onions and lemon grass. Season with sugar, salt and pepper, and add orange juice. Reduce contents of the pan for about 5 minutes and then pour through a fine-mesh strainer. Add mango and purée. Add seasoning to taste and pour a pool of sauce onto 4 appetizer plates. Decoratively arrange crawfish meat on top and garnish with lemon balm leaves.

If desired, drizzle crawfish with a little sherry and heat slightly in the microwave.

Lime Shrimp Tartar with Cilantro Bread

For the cilantro bread: 4 cups flour, 1 pkg dry yeast, 1 pinch sugar,
1 small bunch fresh cilantro, 3 tbs olive oil, Salt
For the tartar: 1 lime, 1 lb shrimp, 1 egg yolk, ¼ tsp Dijon mustard,
⅓ cup olive oil, Salt, Freshly ground black pepper, 1 tbs pickled capers

For the cilantro bread: Sift flour into a bowl and make a well in the center. Pour dry yeast, sugar and ¾ cup lukewarm water into the well, and stir. Dust first-rise dough with a little flour from the edges, cover, and keep in a warm place free of drafts for 20 minutes.

In the meantime, rinse cilantro, pat dry, pluck leaves from stems, chop finely, and mix with olive oil. Knead cilantro oil and salt into the dough, cover, and let rise for another 40 minutes.

For the tartar: Peel lime so that the white outer membrane is also removed, cut segments from between the inner membranes, and chop finely. Combine lime and shrimp and chop very finely. Using an electric hand mixer set to the highest speed, beat egg yolk and mustard until creamy. Gradually beat in olive oil until it forms a mayonnaise. Season with salt and pepper. Stir in shrimp mixture and capers. Refrigerate until needed.

Preheat oven to 425°F. Thoroughly knead dough once more and shape into a loaf. Place on a baking sheet, brush with water, and bake in the oven for 35–40 minutes until crusty. Let bread cool thoroughly before cutting and serve with lime shrimp tartar.

Spaghetti with Lemon Sauce

½ bunch Italian parsley, Juice and grated peel of 1 lemon,
½ lb spaghetti (about 8 oz), Salt, 1 small carrot, 3-4 oz celery root,
3 tbs olive oil, ¼ cup dry white wine, ⅓ cup heavy cream,
½ cup mascarpone cheese, Freshly ground pepper
Plus: 1 peeled lemon

Rinse parsley, pat dry, pluck leaves from stems, and chop finely. Combine parsley, lemon juice, and lemon peel. Place spaghetti in a large pot of boiling, salted water and cook according to package directions until al dente.

In the meantime, peel carrots and celery root and cut into fine strips. Braise briefly in hot olive oil, add wine, and simmer for 5 minutes. Stir in cream and mascarpone and season with salt and pepper.

Drain spaghetti in a colander, pour immediately into a preheated bowl, and toss lightly with sauce and lemon parsley. Transfer to 4 shallow bowls. Cut lemon into small wedges and garnish with lemon wedges.

You can also season with lemon pepper and stir in blanched cherry tomatoes as well as finely chopped arugula.

SALADS

Moroccan Orange Zucchini Salad

1 red onion, 1 lb zucchini, ½ cup pitted dates, 3 oranges, ⅓ cup raisins,
¼ cup olive oil, 1 tsp coarsely crushed coriander seeds, 2 tbs vinegar,
1 pinch ground cinnamon, Salt, Freshly ground black pepper,
¼ cup sliced almonds for garnish

Peel onion, cut in half, and then into strips. Clean zucchini, cut lengthwise into thin slices, and then crosswise into thin strips. Cut dates into thin strips. Peel 2 oranges so that the white outer membrane is also removed and cut segments from between the inner membranes. Squeeze juice from the third orange and pour juice over the raisins.

In a wide pan, heat olive oil and braise onion and zucchini strips for about 5 minutes. Pour the contents of the pan into a bowl and mix with date strips, orange segments, and orange raisins. Season with coriander, vinegar, cinnamon, salt, and pepper, cover and refrigerate for 1 hour. Add seasoning to taste, arrange on plates, and garnish with sliced almonds.

This refreshing salad goes with saffron rice and/or toast with lemon butter. To make the butter, combine softened butter, a little lemon juice, and freshly grated lemon peel. To add an Asian accent, stir in 1 tsp freshly chopped cilantro. Place in individual molds and harden in the refrigerator.

Fruit Salad with Oranges and Pineapple

2 fennel bulbs, 4 oz cooked ham, 2 baby pineapples, 2 oranges,
¾ cup plain yogurt, ¼ tsp curry powder, 1 dash cayenne pepper,
Salt, Freshly ground black pepper, 5 tbs orange juice,
1 tbs chopped parsley, ⅓ cup sliced almonds for garnish

Clean fennel bulbs, cut into quarters, remove core, and cut lengthwise into thin strips. Cut ham into strips. Cut baby pineapples in half lengthwise and cut out fruit, leaving the shells intact for use as decoration later on. Cut about half the pineapple into small pieces (and save the rest for using elsewhere). Peel oranges so that the white outer membrane is also removed and cut segments from between the inner membranes. Combine yogurt, curry, cayenne, salt, pepper, orange juice, and parsley. In a bowl, lightly toss all prepared ingredients with the salad dressing and arrange decoratively in pineapple halves. Garnish the salad with sliced almonds.

 Extreme citrus fruit fans can also add grapefruit and lime segments. In this case, however, be sure to sweeten the dressing.

Arabian Parsley Salad

1 lb beefsteak tomatoes, 2 onions, 1 bunch Italian parsley,
½ cup black olives, Juice of 1 lemon, 1 tsp sugar, ½ cup olive oil,
Salt, Freshly ground black pepper, 1 dash turmeric,
½ tsp cumin, Segments of 1 lemon for garnish

Blanch beefsteak tomatoes, peel, remove cores and seeds, and dice finely. Peel and mince onions. Rinse parsley, pat dry, pluck leaves from stems, and chop finely. Remove pits from olives and cut into strips. In a bowl, combine prepared ingredients, season with lemon juice, sugar, olive oil, salt, pepper, turmeric and cumin, and toss lightly. Cover salad with plastic wrap and refrigerate for at least 1 hour. Serve garnished with lemon segments.

 Goes well with Turkish flatbread.

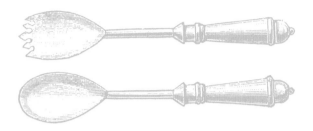

Red Cabbage Salad with Oranges

1 leek, 1 apple, 1 lb red cabbage, Salt, ¼ cup olive oil,
Freshly ground black pepper, 1 pinch sugar, 1 pinch allspice,
2 whole cloves, 1 bay leaf, ½ cup vegetable stock, 1 tbs balsamic vinegar,
1 tbs chopped parsley, 2 oranges, 1 cup chopped walnuts for garnish

Cut leek in half lengthwise, rinse, and cut crosswise into strips. Peel apple, core, and cut into thin slices. Clean red cabbage, remove core, and grate finely with a vegetable grater. Place in a bowl, season with salt, pull apart, and mix thoroughly.

In a deep pan, heat 2 tbs olive oil and briefly braise leek and apple. Season with salt, pepper, sugar, allspice, cloves, and bay leaf. Pour in stock, bring to a boil, and pour mixture over the red cabbage. Season to taste with remaining olive oil, balsamic vinegar, and parsley. Peel orange so that the white outer membrane is also removed and cut segments from between the inner membranes. Mix segments into red cabbage and transfer salad to 4 plates. Serve sprinkled with walnuts.

 Serve either alone or with walnut bread or a baguette, or serve as a side dish with steak or a game ragout.

Fruity Fitness Crudités

2 pink grapefruits, 1 orange, 2 mandarin oranges,
½ lb cauliflower (about 8 oz), 2 pears, 1½ cups plain yogurt,
Salt, Freshly cracked black pepper, 1½ cups watercress

Peel grapefruits and orange so that the white outer membrane is also removed and cut segments from between the inner membranes. Carefully peel mandarin oranges and separate into segments. Arrange ¾ of the fruit on 4 plates in a star pattern.

Clean cauliflower. Peel pears and core. Coarsely grate cauliflower and pears and toss lightly with yogurt. Season with salt and pepper. Spoon this mixture onto the fruit and top with remaining citrus segments. Trim cress stems, rinse, and scatter over fruit.

Great low-calorie, high energy dish. Serve with whole-wheat bread and shaved, grilled ham.

Tenderloin and Orange Bites with Salad

1 lb pork tenderloin, 1 head frisée lettuce, 1 orange, 1 mandarin orange,
Salt, Freshly ground black pepper, ¼ cup pumpkin seed oil,
3 tbs balsamic vinegar, 3 tbs vegetable oil, 1-inch chunk fresh ginger root,
1 shallot, 1 small chile pepper, ⅓ cup apricot jam, Juice of 1 lemon,
1 pinch curry, 1 bag tortilla chips

Cut pork tenderloin into uniform bite-sized cubes. Clean lettuce, rinse, spin dry, and tear into bite-sized pieces. Peel orange and mandarin orange so that the white outer membrane is also removed and cut segments from between the inner membranes. Cut half the segments into small pieces and set aside. Spread lettuce and remaining citrus segments over the surface of 4 plates. Combine pumpkin seed oil, balsamic vinegar, salt and pepper, and drizzle this dressing onto the lettuce.

In a pan, heat vegetable oil and sauté meat cubes on all sides for 3–4 minutes. Transfer to a plate and season with salt and pepper.

Peel and mince ginger and shallot. Remove stem, seeds and interior from chile pepper, and chop finely. In a saucepan, heat apricot jam and lemon juice. Stir in ginger, shallot and chile pepper, and season with curry. Carefully stir in meat and any meat juice that accumulated. Remove meat cubes one at a time, place on top of a tortilla chip, arrange around the edges of the salad plates, and top with orange pieces.

 A somewhat unusual recipe but one of the author's favorite salads. Be sure to try it—bon appetit!

Mussel Mint Salad with Lemon Marinade

1 head butterhead lettuce, ½ bunch fresh mint,
1 jar mussels in water (½ lb drained weight), 2 shallots,
1 cup plain yogurt, Juice of 1 lemon, 1 pinch sugar,
Salt, Freshly ground black pepper, ¼ cup olive oil, 1 orange

Clean lettuce, rinse, spin dry, and cut into strips. Rinse mint, pat dry, pluck leaves from stems, and chop a little finer if necessary. Drain mussels slightly. Peel shallots and cut into strips.

Beat yogurt, lemon juice, sugar, salt, pepper, and olive oil into a smooth dressing. Lightly toss all salad ingredients with the dressing and distribute on 4 plates. Peel orange so that the white outer membrane is also removed and cut segments from between the inner membranes. Garnish salad with orange segments.

 This delicious salad will stimulate dragging spirits. You can also use lemon balm leaves in place of the fresh mint leaves.

Warm Lettuce Salad with Oranges and Shrimp

1 head butterhead lettuce, Salt, 1 clove garlic,
⅔ cup heavy cream, 2 oranges, 6–8 oz peeled shrimp,
Freshly cracked black pepper, 4 slices white bread

Detach lettuce leaves, rinse, and cut crosswise into strips about ½-inch wide. Blanch briefly in boiling, salted water, pour into a colander, rinse under cold water, and drain.

Peel garlic and chop finely. In a wide pot, bring garlic and cream to a boil and simmer for 3–4 minutes. In the meantime, peel orange so that the white outer membrane is also removed, cut segments from between the inner membranes, and toss lightly with the shrimp.

Quickly stir lettuce strips into garlic cream. Season with salt and pepper and remove from heat. Fold in shrimp and orange segments. Add seasoning to taste and decoratively arrange in 4 individual bowls. Toast bread, cut into strips the width of a finger, and stick into the salad as garnish. Serve immediately.

 Other possible garnishes include freshly grated orange zest, freshly chopped parsley, or cress. You can also use smoked salmon in the salad instead of shrimp.

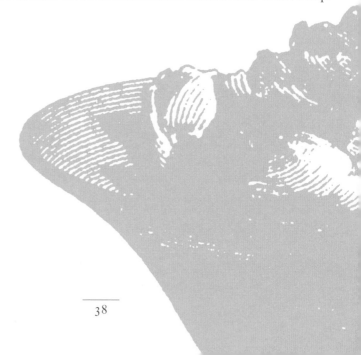

Shrimp Pears with Orange Segments

2 oranges, 5 stalks dill, ¾ cup plain yogurt, ⅓ cup mixed fruit juice,
Juice of ½ lemon, Salt, Freshly ground black pepper,
½ lb peeled shrimp, 2 pears

Peel oranges so that the white outer membrane is also removed and cut segments from between the inner membranes. Rinse dill, pat dry, pluck from stems, and chop finely. Mix half the dill with yogurt, juice, a little lemon juice, salt, and pepper. Fold in shrimp.

Peel pears, cut lengthwise into quarters, core, and cut quarters lengthwise into small, thin slices that are still attached at the bottom end. Arrange 2 pear quarters on each plate and spread into a fan shape. Spoon on shrimp yogurt and garnish with orange segments and chopped dill.

 Goes with grissini wrapped in shaved ham.

39

Breaded Turkey Strips on Orange Yogurt Salad

For the salad: 10 fresh mint leaves or 1 tsp mixed herbs (e.g., parsley,
dill, cress, chervil, chives, sorrel, borage, salad burnet),
1 fennel bulb, 1 orange, 1 small apple, ¾ cup plain yogurt,
Juice of ½ lemon, 1 pinch sugar, Salt, Freshly ground black pepper
For the turkey strips: ½ lb turkey cutlets, Salt,
Freshly ground black pepper, 1 pinch Hungarian sweet paprika,
Flour for dredging, ½ cup finely chopped walnuts,
1 egg, 1 tbs vegetable oil, 1 tbs butter

For the salad: Rinse mint leaves, pat dry, and cut into fine strips. Clean fennel, remove core, and cut into strips. Peel orange so that the white outer membrane is also removed and cut segments from between the inner membranes. Rinse apple, peel, core, and cut into thin wedges.

In a bowl, combine yogurt, mint leaves, lemon juice, sugar, salt and pepper, and toss with fennel, orange segments, and apple wedges.

For the turkey strips: Cut meat into narrow strips and season with salt, pepper, and paprika. Place flour and walnuts in 2 separate shallow bowls. In a third shallow bowl, whisk egg. First dredge turkey strips in flour, then dip in the egg and, finally, dredge in the walnuts. Press breading firmly onto meat.

In a pan, heat vegetable oil and butter. Maintain medium heat to prevent burning. Sauté breaded turkey strips for about 5 minutes, turning several times. Distribute salad on plates and arrange turkey strips on top.

 Serve with an oven-fresh herb baguette or flatbread.

Chicken Salad on Canapés

Makes 2 servings
½ lb grilled chicken, cooked turkey or chicken breast, 1 pink grapefruit,
1 mandarin orange, 1 small can mushroom caps, ½ cup sour cream,
2 tbs mayonnaise, Salt, Freshly ground black pepper,
Hungarian sweet paprika, 4 slices whole-wheat bread

Cut meat into small cubes. Peel grapefruit and mandarin orange so that the white outer membrane is also removed. Cut grapefruit segments from between the inner membranes and separate mandarin orange into segments. Depending on their size, cut mushrooms into halves or quarters.

In a bowl, combine mayonnaise and cream. Lightly fold in grapefruit segments, mandarin orange segments, and poultry cubes. Season with salt, pepper, and paprika. Toast bread, cut diagonally into quarters, and spread with an even layer of salad. Dust with paprika.

This fruity salad is especially good for lunch because its high vitamin C content keeps you from feeling drowsy after the meal. On the contrary, you'll feel ready for anything!

Tropical Fruit Salad with Chicken Breast

*6–8 oz chicken breast, 2 tbs olive oil, 1 carrot, 1 papaya,
1 mango, 1 orange, 1 mandarin orange, 1 pink grapefruit,
1 banana, Juice of 1 lime, 8 large iceberg lettuce leaves
For the dressing: ¾ cup plain yogurt, 1 tsp sugar, Salt,
Freshly ground black pepper, 1 tbs freshly chopped cilantro*

Cut chicken into fine strips. In a pan, heat olive oil and brown meat on all sides for 3–5 minutes, then remove from the pan, and keep warm.

Peel vegetables and fruit and cut everything except carrots and citrus fruits into uniform-sized pieces. Grate carrots and separate citrus fruits into segments. In a large bowl, combine prepared ingredients and drizzle with lime juice. Rinse lettuce leaves and spin dry. Place 1 lettuce leaf on each of 4 plates and cut the rest into strips.

Make a dressing by combining yogurt, sugar, salt, pepper, and cilantro. Add lettuce strips and dressing to other ingredients and toss. Add seasoning to taste and arrange decoratively on the lettuce leaves.

Serve this salad at lunchtime and you'll be in top form. Especially delicious with an oven-fresh baguette or pumpernickel bread.

If you prefer a vegetarian salad: Instead of the chicken, dice 6 oz (herb) tofu, sauté in olive oil on all sides for 3–5 minutes, and mix into the salad.

Roast Beef Salad with Chanterelles

1 small onion, ½ lb fresh chanterelle mushrooms (about 8 oz),
½ lb thinly sliced roast beef, 1 orange, 2 mandarin oranges,
¼ bunch Italian parsley, 3 tbs vegetable oil, Salt,
5 oz mâche (e.g., field salad), 3 tbs walnut oil, 2 tbs sherry vinegar,
1 dash Worcestershire sauce, Freshly ground black pepper

Peel and mince onion. Clean chanterelles and, depending on their size, cut into smaller pieces. Cut roast beef into narrow strips. Peel orange so that the white outer membrane is also removed and cut segments from between the inner membranes. Carefully peel mandarin oranges and separate into segments. Rinse parsley, pat dry, pluck leaves from stems, and chop finely.

In a pan, heat vegetable oil and braise onions until translucent. Add chanterelles and sauté until mushroom liquid has evaporated. In a bowl, combine contents of the pan, roast beef strips, citrus fruits and parsley, and toss lightly.

Clean mâche, then rinse, and spin dry. Combine walnut oil, sherry vinegar and Worcestershire sauce, and mix into the prepared ingredients. Finally, carefully fold in mâche. Season with salt and pepper and arrange decoratively on 4 plates.

 Following a weekend or holiday, there is often leftover roast that can be used in a salad such as this one.

INTERNATIONAL ENTRÉES

Asparagus with Orange Zabaglione

3 lb white asparagus, Salt, 1 pinch sugar, 1 tsp butter, 1 tsp lemon juice
For the zabaglione: 4 egg yolks, 5 tbs orange juice, Salt,
Freshly ground black pepper, Several drops Worcestershire sauce,
1 tsp freshly chopped cilantro, ¼ cup ricotta cheese, 3 tbs melted butter
Plus: 2 oranges for garnish

Rinse asparagus spears, peel, and cook in a large amount of water seasoned with salt, sugar, butter, and lemon juice for about 15 minutes until al dente. Transfer asparagus to preheated plates and keep warm, leaving the cooking water on the burner.

For the zabaglione: Combine egg yolks, orange juice, and 5 tbs asparagus water in a heat-resistant bowl. Place bowl over the hot steam of the asparagus pot and beat ingredients until you have a thick foam.

Remove bowl from double boiler, beat briefly over ice water, and season with salt, freshly ground pepper, Worcestershire sauce, and cilantro. Gradually beat in cream ricotta and butter.

Peel oranges so that the white outer membrane is also removed and cut segments from between the inner membranes. Spoon zabaglione onto the asparagus and garnish with orange segments.

🍊 Goes with new potatoes, but also with potato pancakes or white bread dunked in the zabaglione. As a finishing touch, heat 2 tbs orange liqueur (e.g., Grand Marnier) in a soup ladle, light it, and use it to flambé the asparagus servings.

Lemon Tuna on Tomato Sauce

4 slices tuna (about 5–6 oz each), 4 lemons, Salt,
Freshly ground black pepper, 1 onion, 2 cloves garlic, ⅓ cup olive oil,
¾ cup dry white wine, 8 oz canned, diced Roma tomatoes,
½ bunch Italian parsley

Rinse tuna slices under cold running water, pat dry with paper towels, and spread out on a platter. Squeeze juice from 2 lemons and drizzle juice over the fish slices. Season with salt and pepper.

Peel and mince onion and garlic. In a pan, heat 3 tbs olive oil and braise onion and garlic until translucent. Pour in white wine and stir in tomatoes. Season with salt and pepper and simmer gently for 5 minutes.

In the meantime, heat remaining olive oil in a second pan and sauté tuna slices for about 3 minutes on each side, then continue cooking gently over low heat.

Rinse parsley, pat dry, pluck leaves from stems, chop finely, and add to tomato sauce. Peel remaining 2 lemons so that the white outer membrane is also removed, cut segments from between the inner membranes, and cut into smaller pieces if desired. Once again, season sauce to taste and distribute on 4 preheated plates. Place 1 tuna slice on top of each and garnish with lemon pieces.

 There are 3 steps to preparing fish: Cleaning, acidifying, and salting. Note: The acid must come before the salt. This seals up the fish so it fries better.

Baked Fish Fillet with Root Vegetables

4 frozen fish fillets (e.g., snapper), Juice of 2 limes,
Salt, Freshly ground black pepper,
Assorted soup vegetables (1 carrot, 1 stalk celery with greens,
2 green onions), ¼ cup parsley, 2 tbs butter,
1 cup heavy cream, 1 tbs butter cut into bits

Thaw fish fillets, rinse under cold water, pat dry, drizzle with the juice of 1 lime, and season with salt and pepper. Peel or clean soup vegetables and cut into fine strips. Rinse parsley, pat dry, pluck leaves from stems, and chop finely.

Preheat oven to 400°F. In a pan, heat 1 tbs butter and braise vegetable strips for 3–4 minutes until translucent. Combine contents of the pan, remaining lime juice and parsley, and pour into a shallow casserole dish. Place fish fillets on top, pour on cream, and top with remaining butter cut into bits. Cover casserole dish with aluminum foil and bake in the oven for 25–30 minutes. For the last 10 minutes, bake without foil.

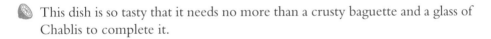 This dish is so tasty that it needs no more than a crusty baguette and a glass of Chablis to complete it.

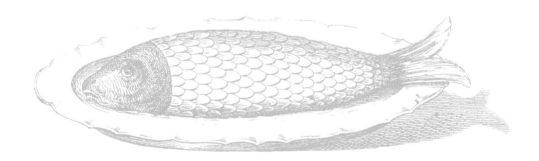

Cheese Fondue with a Light Citrus Accompaniment

For the fondue: 1 clove garlic, 8 oz Gruyère cheese,
1 cup dry white wine, Juice of 1 lemon, 1 tbs flour or cornstarch,
8 oz Vacherin (special fondue cheese),
1 tbs orange liqueur (e.g., Grand Marnier)
Plus: 6–8 oz mushrooms, 2 oranges, 2 grapefruits, 2 mandarin oranges,
8 oz thinly sliced, cooked ham, 1 large baguette

Clean mushrooms and, depending on their size, cut in half or leave whole. Peel oranges and grapefruits so that the white outer membrane is also removed and cut segments from between the inner membranes. Carefully peel mandarin oranges and separate into segments. Cut ham slices into strips and wrap around some of the citrus segments.

In a small bowl, combine all prepared ingredients and place in the center of the table. Cut baguette into uniform bite-sized pieces and place in a bread basket.

For the fondue: Cut garlic clove in half and rub cut sides around inside a caquelon (a special ceramic pot for cheese fondue). Grate Gruyère very finely. In a saucepan, combine Gruyère and white wine. Stir lemon juice into flour until smooth and drizzle over the cheese. Finely grate Vacherin and sprinkle over the top. Flavor with orange liqueur. Melt cheese mixture in the saucepan on the stove, then pour into the fondue pot, and place it on an alcohol burner.

Depending on your taste, dip fennel pieces, cherry tomatoes, radishes, or zucchini pieces into the cheese. Or dip bread pieces into the cheese and then roll them around in chopped parsley or cress. This makes the "fatty" cheese much easier to digest. And if you drink black tea with cheese fondue, you won't need a digestif after the meal. But you can still have one if you want!

Nonstick fondue pots are now available that can be placed on an electrically heated base on the table. You can heat the cheese in this pot directly on the stove. The advantage is that you don't have to transfer the mixture to another pot.

Mandarin Pork and Rice

½ lb pork tenderloin (about 8 oz), Salt, Freshly ground black pepper,
1 onion, 2 cloves garlic, 5 tbs vegetable oil,
1¼ cups long-grain rice (about 8 oz), 1 pinch cayenne pepper,
⅓ cup dry white wine, 2¼ cups meat stock, ¾ cup sliced almonds,
2 peach halves (canned), 1 small can mandarin oranges,
2 tbs mango chutney (prepared product)

Cut pork tenderloin into narrow strips and season with salt and pepper. Peel and mince onion and garlic. In a wide pot, heat 2 tbs vegetable oil, brown tenderloin strips on all sides, and transfer to a plate.

In a saucepan, heat remaining vegetable oil and braise onion and garlic until translucent. Stir in rice and season with cayenne, salt, and pepper. Add white wine and meat stock and bring to a boil. Stir in pork strips with any meat juice that accumulated, cover, and simmer over medium heat for about 20 minutes. In the meantime, toast sliced almonds in a hot, ungreased pan until they start to give off an aroma and transfer to a plate.

Cut peach halves into strips. Drain mandarin oranges, saving the juice. Stir juice into mango chutney. Just before the meat and rice dish is done cooking, lightly stir in chutney and fruit. Distribute on preheated plates and sprinkle with almonds.

 Goes with a lettuce salad with orange segments and vinaigrette.

Meat and Vegetable Broil with Lemon Sauce

1 small eggplant, Salt, 1 fennel bulb, 2 beefsteak tomatoes,
½ bunch mixed fresh herbs (e.g., oregano, thyme, basil), 4 lamb chop,
4 pork medallions (about 3 oz each), Freshly ground black pepper,
4 cloves garlic, Juice of 1 lemon, 5–8 tbs olive oil
For the sauce: 3 egg yolks, ¼ tsp hot mustard, ⅓ cup olive oil, Salt,
Coarsely cracked black pepper, 1 pinch sugar, Juice of ½ lemon

Clean eggplant, cut lengthwise into quarters, and soak in cold, salted water for 15 minutes. Clean fennel bulb, cut into quarters, and remove core. Chop fennel greens coarsely and set aside for the sauce. Rinse tomatoes, remove cores, and cut in half crosswise. Rinse mixed herbs, pat dry, and spread on a baking sheet. Season meat pieces on both sides with salt and pepper and place on the bed of herbs. Peel garlic and chop finely. Thoroughly mix garlic, lemon juice, and olive oil.

Preheat oven to 400°F. Remove eggplant from salted water and sponge dry with paper towels. Distribute eggplant, fennel, and tomatoes on the bed of herbs. Season lightly with salt and pepper. Drizzle lemon oil over the vegetables and meat. Cook meat and vegetables in the oven for 30 minutes, turning 2–3 times. During the last 10 minutes, switch on the broiler.

For the sauce: Using an electric hand mixer set to the highest speed, beat egg yolks and mustard until thick and creamy. Gradually beat in olive oil until the sauce takes on a creamy consistency. Season with fennel greens, salt, pepper, sugar, and lemon juice.

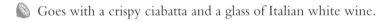 Goes with a crispy ciabatta and a glass of Italian white wine.

Citrus Beef Baskets

*¾ cup pine nuts, 4 large oranges, 1 onion, 2 cloves garlic, 5 tbs olive oil,
10 oz ground beef, ½ tsp thyme, stripped, 1 large pinch cinnamon,
1 pinch cayenne pepper, 1 bay leaf, Salt, Freshly cracked black pepper*

Heat an ungreased pan and toast pine nuts until they begin to give off an aroma, then transfer to a plate.

Rinse oranges under hot water, dry with paper towels, and cut in half crosswise. Hollow out peel halves and set aside. Cut ¼ of the fruit into small pieces and set a side with a little of the juice that escaped (use remaining fruit for another dish, such as a dessert). Peel and mince onion and garlic. Heat olive oil and braise onion and garlic until translucent. Add ground meat and sauté while stirring until crumbly. Season with thyme, cinnamon, cayenne, bay leaf, salt, and pepper. Sauté over medium heat for about 10 minutes until done. Then stir in orange pieces and juice and add seasoning to taste.

Fill orange peel halves with ground meat mixture. Sprinkle with a thick layer of pine nuts and arrange 2 orange baskets on each plate.

Wiener Schnitzel

I wouldn't touch a Wiener Schnitzel unless I had fresh lemons in the house. Just imagine paper-thin slices of pounded veal, preferably cut from the leg, with a crispy fried breadcrumb coating slightly raised from the meat in places, served on preheated plates with parsley, and lemon wedges. Rapturously drizzle fresh lemon juice over the top and just before taking the first bite, close your eyes and experience the symbiosis of crispness and lemony freshness…

4 thin veal cutlets (about 6 oz each), Salt, Freshly ground black pepper,
Flour for dredging, Freshly grated breadcrumbs, 2 eggs,
2 tbs heavy cream or milk, About 1 cup vegetable oil for frying,
2 lemons, 4 stalks curly-leaved parsley

Gently pound veal cutlets with a steak hammer. Season on both sides with salt and pepper. Place flour and breadcrumbs in 2 separate shallow bowls. In a third shallow bowl, beat eggs with cream or milk. First dredge cutlets in flour, then dip in the eggs and, finally, dredge several times in the breadcrumbs without pressing the breading onto the meat.

In 2 medium-sized pans or 1 large pan, heat oil and fry cutlets on both sides until crispy. Reduce heat and fry meat for another 2–3 minutes until done, basting several times with the fat. Remove and, if desired, drain briefly on paper towels. Arrange on plates and garnish with lemon wedges and parsley sprigs.

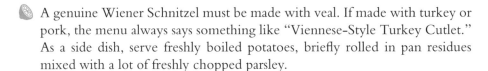 A genuine Wiener Schnitzel must be made with veal. If made with turkey or pork, the menu always says something like "Viennese-Style Turkey Cutlet." As a side dish, serve freshly boiled potatoes, briefly rolled in pan residues mixed with a lot of freshly chopped parsley.

Lemon Schnitzel with Chard

1 small onion, 2 cloves garlic, 1 lb chard, 2 tbs butter, Sea salt,
Freshly ground black pepper, 4 thin veal cutlets (about 5–6 oz each),
¼ cup olive oil, ⅓ cup heavy cream, ¼ cup herb crème fraîche,
1 pinch freshly ground nutmeg, Juice of 1 lemon

Peel and mince onion and garlic. Clean chard, rinse, and cut leaves crosswise into strips about ½-inch wide. In a wide pot, heat butter and braise onion and garlic until translucent. Add chard strips and braise for another 5 minutes. Season with salt and pepper.

Pound veal cutlets flat and season with pepper. In a pan, heat olive oil and sauté cutlets for 2 minutes on each side. Remove and season with salt.

Enrich chard mixture with cream, herb crème fraîche, and nutmeg. Transfer cutlets to 4 preheated plates and drizzle with lemon juice. Arrange chard beside the veal.

 If the season permits, briefly sear the pounded veal cutlets on a very hot charcoal grill, drizzle with lemon juice, and serve. If you need a sauce, simply make up a mayonnaise and refine it with lemon juice and lemon zest.

Brazilian Orange Beef Tenderloin

2 lb beef tenderloin, 3 cloves garlic, ½ tsp salt, ¼ tsp cinnamon,
¼ tsp cumin, Freshly cracked black pepper,
5 tbs vegetable oil, 2 oranges, 1 lime

Trim all but a thin layer of fat from the beef tenderloin. Rinse meat under cold water, pat dry with paper towels, and pierce several times all the way around with a fork.

Peel garlic and squeeze through a press. Combine garlic, salt, cinnamon, cumin, pepper, and 2 tbs vegetable oil to form a paste. Rub into beef tenderloin on all sides.

Preheat oven to 400°F. In a roasting pan, heat remaining vegetable oil and brown tenderloin on all sides. Place broiler pan in the oven and cook roast for up to 40 minutes, turning several times. Remove meat, wrap in aluminum foil, and let stand for 10 minutes.

In the meantime, rinse oranges under hot water, dry thoroughly with paper towels, and use a zester to remove thin strips of orange zest. Squeeze juice from lime and drizzle juice onto zest. Then peel both oranges so that the white outer membrane is also removed and cut the fruit into thin slices.

Unwrap meat and slice thinly. Pour meat juice into a gravy boat. Arrange orange and meat slices in an overlapping pattern on a large platter. Drizzle with lime juice, sprinkle with orange zest, cover with aluminum foil, and marinate in the refrigerator for 2 hours. Serve cold with the meat juice on the side.

 Goes with homemade mayonnaise flavored with orange juice and a lot of crusty baguette.

Ribeye Steak with Grapefruit Condiment

*1 pink grapefruit, 4 ribeye beef steaks (about 6 oz each),
¼ cup vegetable oil, Salt, Freshly cracked black pepper,
½ cup chopped walnuts*

Peel grapefruit so that the white outer membrane is also removed and cut segments from between the inner membranes. Flatten steaks slightly with the palm of your hand. In a pan, heat vegetable oil and sauté meat slices for 3–4 minutes on each side. Season with salt and pepper. Transfer to a plate, cover with aluminum foil, and set aside. Add grapefruit segments to pan residues, stir for 1–2 minutes, and salt lightly.

Place steaks on 4 plates. Return any meat juice that accumulated to the pan of grapefruit segments. Stir around the contents of the pan once more and pour over the meat. Garnish with chopped walnuts.

 Goes with potatoes au gratin and a tossed salad.

Grilled Pork Shoulder Steaks with Shallot Lime Sauce

*6 shallots, Juice of 3 limes, Salt, 1 red chile pepper, 4 garlic cloves,
2 tbs butter, 4 pork shoulder steaks, Salt, Freshly ground black pepper,
½ tsp grilling spice (your favorite prepared product), ¼ cup vegetable oil*

Peel shallots and cut into fine strips. In a bowl, combine shallots, lime juice, and 1 pinch salt. Cover with plastic wrap and set aside for 30 minutes.

In the meantime, remove stem, seeds and interior from chile pepper, and chop finely. Peel and mince garlic. Drain shallots in a sieve, setting aside juice.

In a pan, heat butter and add shallot strips, chile pepper, and garlic. Braise for about 20 minutes, stirring repeatedly. Pour the contents of the pan into a bowl and mix with the set aside lime juice.

Season pork shoulder steaks with salt, pepper, and grill spices. In a pan, heat oil and sauté steaks for 5 minutes on each side, or cook on a very hot charcoal grill until both sides are crispy. Transfer 1 steak to each plate and top with a little shallot lime sauce.

 Instead of shallots, use onions and increase the chile peppers as desired. Suitable side dishes include grilled corn on the cob and foil-wrapped potatoes.

Pork Medallions on Toast with Orange Banana Sauce

1¼ lb pork tenderloin, 2 tbs vegetable oil,
Salt, Freshly ground black pepper, 4 slices sandwich bread
For the sauce: 2 bananas, Juice of 1 orange and ½ lime, 1 tbs mango
chutney (prepared product), ¾ cup sour cream, ¼ tsp curry powder,
Salt, Freshly ground black pepper, 1 tsp brown sugar
Plus: Segments of 1 orange

For the sauce: Peel bananas and mash with a fork. Combine bananas, orange juice, and lime juice. Gradually stir in remaining sauce ingredients, cover with plastic wrap, and refrigerate.

In the meantime, cut pork tenderloin crosswise into 8 medallions and flatten slightly with the palm of your hand. In a pan, heat oil and sauté medallions for 4–6 minutes on each side. Season with salt and pepper.

Toast bread slices, spread with a thin layer of banana sauce, and top each slice with 2 medallions. Cover with remaining sauce and garnish with orange segments.

You can vary the sauce as desired by adding sliced almonds and freshly chopped parsley.

Instead of the sauce described here, you can also use the Mandarin-Scented Banana Sauce (see recipe on page 79).

Smoked Pork Loin Toast with Oranges and Bananas

4 smoked pork loin chops without bones, Meat stock (optional),
4 slices white bread, 1 tbs cold butter, 2 oranges,
4 oz freshly grated cheese (e.g., Gouda), 1½ cups cornflakes,
1 tbs melted butter, 1 dash curry powder, 1 banana, Juice of ½ lemon

Heat loin chops in hot water or hot stock, or microwave for 4–5 minutes. Toast bread slices and spread with butter. Peel oranges so that the white outer membrane is also removed and cut segments from between the inner membranes. Combine cheese, cornflakes, melted butter and curry, and toss lightly. Preheat oven to 400°F.

Place 1 loin chop on each toasted bread slice and place on a baking sheet. Peel banana, slice, drizzle with lemon juice, and distribute on loin chops along with the orange segments. Top with cornflake-cheese mixture. Place baking sheet in the preheated oven, switch to the broiler setting, and broil for up to 10 minutes until crispy.

 Instead of the smoked pork loin, you can use fast-cooking cuts of meat (e.g., pork tenderloin, flattened chicken breast fillet, thick slices of Canadian bacon). As a side dish, serve either a mâche salad with vinaigrette, bacon and walnuts, or an iceberg lettuce salad with yogurt dressing.

Turkey Tenders in Mandarin Orange Cream

1 lb turkey cutlets, Freshly ground black pepper, 1 tsp dried oregano,
1 onion, 1 clove garlic, 1 small can mandarin oranges, 3 tbs olive oil,
Salt, 1 tbs butter, 3 tbs Marsala (Italian dessert wine),
¼ cup dry white wine, 1 cup heavy cream, 2 tbs apricot jam,
1 pinch cayenne pepper

Cut turkey cutlets into narrow strips and season with pepper and oregano. Peel and mince onion and garlic. Drain off half the juice from the mandarin oranges.

In a large pan, heat olive oil and sear meat strips on all sides in several batches. Transfer to a plate and season with salt. Heat butter in the pan residues and braise onion and garlic until translucent. Add Marsala, white wine, and cream. Stir in jam and reduce sauce for 3–5 minutes. Season with salt, pepper, and cayenne. Stir in mandarin oranges with remaining juice, meat strips, and any meat juice that accumulated. Add seasoning to taste and serve immediately.

- For garnish, offer beautifully decorated orange slices: Stir a little apricot jam into whipped cream and spoon dollops onto orange slices.

- Instead of canned mandarin oranges, you can also use fragrant, fresh mandarin oranges. However, the canned mandarin oranges are sweeter and juicier, which is why I prefer using them in this particular dish.

Viennese-Style Fried Chicken

2 cleaned chickens (about 2¼ lb each), Juice of ½ lemon,
Salt, Freshly ground black pepper, Flour for dredging,
Freshly grated breadcrumbs for coating, 3 eggs,
3 tbs milk, 1 cup vegetable oil, ⅓ cup butter, 2 lemons

Cut each chicken into 4 parts, remove skin, and debone. Rinse chicken pieces and pat dry. Drizzle with lemon juice and season with salt and pepper. Place flour and breadcrumbs in 2 separate shallow bowls. In a third shallow bowl, whisk eggs with milk. First dredge chicken pieces in flour, then dip in the eggs and, finally, dredge in the breadcrumbs.

In a large pan or 2 medium-sized pans, heat butter and sauté chicken pieces on all side for about 15 minutes until crispy, while constantly basting with the cooking fat.

If desired, drain on paper towels and arrange on plates. Cut lemons into quarters or eighths and serve with the chicken.

 What I most want to emphasize about this recipe: What would fried chicken be without lemon juice to drizzle over it? And what a specialty it is with it!

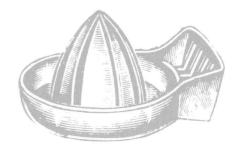

Lemon Rosemary Chicken

2 cleaned chickens (about 2¼ lb each), 4 shallots, 4 cloves garlic,
½ cup olive oil, 3–4 branches fresh rosemary, Juice of 2 lemons
For the lemon butter: ½ cup softened butter (1 stick), Juice of 1 lemon,
Salt, Freshly ground black pepper,
Lemon zest and/or lemon pepper (optional)

Cut each chicken into 4 parts, rinse, and pat dry. Peel shallots and cut into strips. Peel garlic, squeeze through a press, and combine with olive oil. Rinse rosemary, pat dry, strip leaves from the stems, and chop finely. Beat the rosemary with lemon juice and olive oil. In a casserole dish, mix chicken pieces with lemon-garlic oil, cover with plastic wrap, and refrigerate for about 2 hours.

In the meantime, make the lemon butter: Combine butter and lemon juice and season with salt and pepper. If desired, stir in freshly grated lemon zest and/or lemon pepper. Transfer butter to 4 individual molds and refrigerate.

Preheat oven to 400°F. Remove plastic wrap from casserole dish and place chicken in the oven. Bake for about 30 minutes, turning several times in the process. For the last 10 minutes, switch on the broiler. Serve chicken with lemon butter on the side.

 Delicious with flatbread, which you can also dip into the exquisite oil from the casserole dish. As a side dish, serve cubes of feta cheese mixed with black and green olives.

Chicken Skewers on Orange Rice

1 lb chicken breast fillets, 1 tbs garam masala (Indian spice mixture),
2 tbs olive oil, Juice of 2 limes, Salt, Freshly ground black pepper
For the orange rice: ⅓ cup butter, 1¼ cups long-grain rice,
Salt, Freshly ground black pepper, 1 pinch sugar,
3 pinches ground saffron, 1 tsp black caraway seeds,
2⅓ cups vegetable stock, 2 oranges,
¾ cup slivered almonds, ¾ cup raisins
Plus: 4 shish kebab skewers

Cut chicken into narrow strips. In a bowl, mix chicken with garam masala, olive oil, lime juice, 1 pinch salt, and 1 pinch pepper.

For the orange rice: In a wide pot, heat butter and stir in rice. Season with salt, pepper, sugar, saffron, and black caraway seeds. Pour in stock, bring to a boil and cook rice over medium heat for 10 minutes.

In the meantime, peel orange so that the white outer membrane is also removed and cut segments from between the inner membranes. Add orange segments, slivered almonds, and raisins to the rice. Cover the pot with a lid, remove from heat, and let stand for 15 minutes.

In the meantime, thread meat pieces evenly onto each skewer. In a hot, nonstick pan, sauté meat skewers on all sides without adding any oil for 5−8 minutes until crispy. Distribute orange rice on 4 preheated plates and place 1 skewer on top of each serving.

This is an ideal dish for summer. You can also serve the orange rice cold as a salad. And, of course, chicken skewers cooked on a charcoal grill taste better than those from a pan.

Garam masala is an Indian spice mixture that you can buy as a prepared product, or you can quickly make your own. In a mortar, crush 1 tsp each of whole cloves, cumin seeds, cardamom seeds, and black peppercorns. Then add 1 tsp nutmeg and 1 tsp cinnamon. Store in an airtight jar.

Chicken Livers with Mandarin Oranges and Pineapple

1 lb chicken livers, Freshly ground black pepper, 2 tbs flour,
5 tbs vegetable oil, Salt, About ½ cup gravy,
1 small can mandarin oranges,
4 oz (about ½ cup) pineapple chunks (canned),
1 tbs chopped parsley

Rinse chicken livers, pat dry with paper towels, and cut into strips. Season with pepper and dredge only lightly in flour. In a pan, heat vegetable oil and sauté liver strips on all sides for 3–4 minutes. Transfer to a plate and season with salt.

Pour meat juice from the pan into a measuring cup and add canned gravy until you have about ⅔ cup. Pour back into the pan and briefly bring to a boil. Drain mandarin oranges and pineapple chunks and add wet fruit to the pan. Stir briefly, season to taste with salt and pepper and then add liver strips and any meat juice that accumulated. Immediately transfer to plates and garnish with parsley.

Goes with orange-colored mashed potatoes: Boil potatoes, peel, mash, and combine with melted butter, 1 tsp tomato paste, and herb crème fraîche.

Roast Goose with Orange Sauce

Makes 7–8 servings
1 cleaned goose (about 10 lb), Salt, Freshly ground black pepper,
Hungarian sweet paprika, ½ cup meat stock,
2 tbs orange liqueur (e.g., Grand Marnier)
For the stuffing: 5 oranges, 2 sugar cubes, 1 tbs honey, 4 apples,
⅓–½ cup raisins, 2 tbs sherry, 1 day-old (about 6 inch) bread roll,
½ cup slivered almonds, 1 tsp dried marjoram, 1 cup boiling water
Plus: Metal or wooden skewers, or kitchen string

Rinse goose thoroughly inside and out under cold running water. Rub dry with a kitchen towel and season inside and out with salt, pepper, and paprika.

For the stuffing: Peel 4 oranges so that the white outer membrane is also removed and cut segments from between the inner membranes. Grate peel from remaining orange. Cut orange in half, squeeze out juice, pour juice through a fine-mesh strainer, and combine with honey. Set aside sugar cubes, grated orange peel, and orange juice. Peel apples, core, and cut into eighths. Pour sherry over raisins. Dice bread roll. Combine half the orange segments, apple pieces, raisins, bread cubes, slivered almonds and marjoram, and stuff the mixture loosely into the goose cavity. Close cavity with metal or wooden skewers, or sew shut with kitchen string.

Preheat oven to 400°F. Pierce goose several times on all sides with a fork, place in a suitably sized roasting pan and pour boiling water over the top. Place pan on the bottom oven rack. After roasting for about 1 hour, turn goose. At the same time, remove accumulated fat with a ladle and pour in ½ cup boiling hot water. After roasting for another 1½ hours, brush goose with half the orange juice that was set aside, and switch on the broiler until the goose is browned to the desired degree.

When the goose is done, remove it from the roasting pan, cover with aluminum foil, and let stand for 10 minutes. Strain meat juice into a saucepan, add meat stock, and boil uncovered for 10 minutes. Stir in remaining orange juice, peel, and liqueur. Season to taste with salt and pepper and let gravy stand briefly.

Cut goose into 8 pieces and arrange on a platter. Transfer stuffing to a bowl. Stir remaining orange segments into the gravy and pour into a gravy boat. Serve stuffing and gravy on the side.

 The traditional side dishes are red cabbage and dumplings. Because goose is often very fatty, it is commonly prepared with fruits such as apples and oranges and with spices that make it easier to digest.

Chicken Curry with Limes and Lemon Grass

1 lb chicken breast fillets, Juice of 1 lime, 2 small chile peppers, 1 stalk lemon grass, 3 tbs vegetable oil, 3 tbs green curry paste, 2¼ cups unsweetened coconut milk (canned), ½ cup chicken stock, 8 kaffir lime leaves, 2 tbs Thai fish sauce, Salt and freshly ground black pepper as needed, 2 tbs chopped cilantro

Cut chicken breast fillets into strips and drizzle with lime juice. Remove stems, seeds and interiors from chile peppers, and cut in half lengthwise. Clean lemon grass and cut in half crosswise.

In a wok or suitably sized pan, heat oil and stir-fry curry paste. Add coconut milk and stock and bring to a boil. Stir in chile peppers, kaffir lime leaves and lemon grass stalk, and simmer uncovered over medium heat for 5 minutes.

Stir in chicken strips and cook gently over low heat for 5–8 minutes. Season to taste with fish sauce and, if necessary, season with salt and pepper (caution: the fish sauce is very salty!). Remove lime leaves and lemon grass. Sprinkle with curry and cilantro and serve.

 This fiery curry leaves a pleasant sweet-and-sour aftertaste. You will find the ingredients in any well-stocked Asian store or in the specialty foods department of a large department store.

 The only way to soothe your burning tongue is with coconut milk, sugar, or plain yogurt because capsaicin, the spicy ingredient contained in chile peppers, is not water-soluble. This is why water only alleviates the burning temporarily without actually neutralizing it.

Lime Chicken with Olives

*2 cleaned chickens (about 2¼ lb each), Salt, Freshly ground black pepper,
1 small chile pepper, 2 onions, 2 cloves garlic, 5 oz black olives,
½ bunch fresh mint, ½ bunch fresh parsley, ⅓ cup olive oil,
¼ tsp brown sugar, Juice of 2 limes*

Cut each chicken into 4 parts, rinse, and pat dry with paper towels. Season on all sides with salt and pepper. Remove stem, seeds and interior from chile pepper, and mince. Peel onions and garlic and cut into strips. Remove pits from olives and cut into strips. Rinse herbs. pat dry, pluck leaves from stems, and chop finely.

In a bowl, combine chile pepper, onions, garlic, olives, herbs, olive oil, sugar and lime juice, and mix with chicken pieces. Cover with plastic wrap and marinate in the refrigerator for 2 hours.

Preheat oven to 425°F. Pour chicken and marinade into a casserole dish and bake on the center rack of the oven for 50 minutes, turning several times in the process. Remove from the oven and serve in the casserole dish.

 Goes with foil-wrapped potatoes, which also let you take advantage of the hot oven.

Caribbean Pineapple Chicken

2 cleaned chickens (about 2¼ lb each), Salt, Freshly ground black pepper,
2 oranges, 1 small red chili pepper, 4 green onions, 4 shallots,
½ bunch cilantro, 1 cup pineapple chunks (canned), Juice of 1 lime,
1 tsp dried thyme, 1 tbs Worcestershire sauce, 4 tbs white rum,
3 tbs vegetable oil, 1 tbs brown sugar,
1 cup chicken stock, 2 tbs tomato ketchup

Cut each chicken into 4 parts, rinse, and pat dry with paper towels. Season on all sides with salt and pepper. Peel oranges so that the white outer membrane is also removed and cut segments from between the inner membranes. Remove stem, seeds and interior from chile pepper, and mince. Clean green onions and chop finely. Peel and mince shallots. Rinse cilantro, pat dry, pluck leaves from stems, and chop finely.

Combine orange segments, chile pepper, green onions, shallots, cilantro, pineapple chunks, lime juice, thyme, Worcestershire sauce and rum, and mix with chicken pieces. Cover with plastic wrap and marinate in the refrigerator for about 1 hour.

Remove chicken from marinade and pat dry with paper towels. In a wide, deep pan, heat vegetable oil and melt sugar.

Place chicken in the pan, brown on all sides, and remove. Stir stock and ketchup into pan residues and bring to a boil. Add chicken pieces and marinade, cover, and cook over medium heat for 35–40 minutes.

 Goes with fried potatoes or yams. Marinating time is stated as 1 hour. If you want your chicken to have a more intense flavor, you can marinate it for up to 24 hours.

Baked Lamb Chops on a Bed of Lemons

4 lemons, 2 cloves garlic, ½ cup olive oil,
½ cup dried tomatoes in olive oil, ½ bunch fresh thyme,
2 slices white bread without crusts,
½ cup freshly grated Parmesan cheese, loosely packed,
12 small lamb chops, Salt, Freshly ground black pepper
Plus: Juice of ½ lemon

Preheat oven to 400°F. Rinse lemons, wipe dry, and slice. Peel garlic, squeeze through a press, and stir into 5 tbs olive oil.

Line the bottom of a large, shallow casserole dish with lemon slices and drizzle with garlic oil. Heat in the oven for 15–20 minutes.

In the meantime, drain dried tomatoes and chop finely. Rinse thyme, pat dry, pluck leaves from stems, and chop finely. Crumble or grate bread coarsely and combine with tomatoes, thyme, Parmesan, and 1 tbs olive oil.

In a large pan, heat remaining olive oil and brown lamb chops for 1 minute on each side. Season with salt and pepper and arrange side by side on the lemon slices in the casserole dish. Spread a little tomato-thyme paste on each lamb chop.

Return casserole dish to the oven and bake for 10–12 minutes. Remove, drizzle with lemon juice, and serve immediately.

Goes with small potatoes baked with olive oil, salt, and pepper. These potatoes are especially delicious if you cut a slit in each one and insert a bay leaf.

Lamb Kebab with Lemon Pilaf

For the lamb kebabs: 1 orange, 1 lemon, 1 onion, 1 clove garlic,
⅓ cup olive oil, 2 bay leaves, ¼ tsp cinnamon, ½ tsp cumin,
1 large pinch cayenne pepper, 1½ lb lamb fillets,
Salt, Freshly ground black pepper
For the Pilaf: ¾ cup raisins, Juice of 1 orange, 2 cloves garlic,
5 tbs olive oil, 1¼ cups long-grain rice,
Salt, Freshly ground black pepper, ¼ tsp saffron threads,
2⅓ cups vegetable stock, 2 lemons
Plus: 8 shish kebab skewers

For the lamb kebabs: Squeeze juice from orange and lemon. Peel and mince onion and garlic. In a small bowl, combine onion, garlic, orange juice, lemon juice, olive oil, bay leaves, cinnamon, cumin, and cayenne. Depending on their size, cut lamb fillets crosswise into halves or thirds. In a bowl, mix lamb with marinade, cover, and marinate in the refrigerator for at least 12 hours.

Drain marinated lamb in a colander, setting aside the marinade. Thread meat pieces onto 8 skewers.

For the pilaf: In a small bowl, pour orange juice over raisins. Peel and mince garlic. In a saucepan, heat olive oil and briefly braise garlic until translucent. Sprinkle in rice and sauté for 1 minute while stirring. Season with salt, pepper and saffron, and add stock. Cover the saucepan and simmer over medium heat for about 10 minutes, then remove from heat. Rinse lemon under hot water, wipe dry, cut into quarters, and add to the rice. Replace the cover and let rice stand for 20 minutes.

Brush marinade onto lamb kebabs. In a hot, nonstick pan, sauté skewers on all sides without adding any oil for 6–8 minutes until crispy and season with salt and pepper. Remove lemon quarters from rice. Distribute rice on 4 plates and place 2 lamb kebabs on top of each.

 These kebabs taste even better cooked over a charcoal grill.

Duck in Orange Sauce

1 cleaned duck (about 3 lb), Salt, Freshly ground black pepper,
¼ cup vegetable oil, ½ cup hot meat stock, 2 oranges,
⅓ cup sugar, 2 tbs white wine vinegar, 1 tsp cornstarch,
2 tbs Cointreau (orange liqueur)

Preheat oven to 400°F. Rinse duck inside and out under cold running water. Pat dry with paper towels and season inside and out with salt and pepper. Place a roasting pan on the stove, heat vegetable oil, and brown duck on all sides. Place pan on the bottom oven rack. Cook for about 1 hour, turning duck several times in the process and basting with the boiling hot stock.

In the meantime, rinse oranges under hot water and wipe dry with paper towels. Using a zester, grate very fine zest from about 1½ oranges. Cut both oranges in half, squeeze out juice, and pour through a fine-mesh strainer.

When the duck is done, remove it from the roasting pan and wrap in aluminum foil. Return roasting pan to the stovetop and loosen pan residues by simmering 1 cup water. Pour sauce through a fine-mesh strainer. In a saucepan, combine orange zest and sugar and melt over low heat while stirring. Add orange juice and vinegar and pour into strained sauce. Stir cornstarch into 2 tbs water until smooth and stir into boiling sauce. Add seasoning to taste and refine with orange liqueur and orange zest.

Remove duck from foil. Pour any meat juice that accumulated into the sauce and cut meat into 4 pieces. Arrange meat on preheated plates and pour sauce all around it.

 For garnish, top freshly cut orange slices with cranberry sauce or try some orange marmalade.

Rabbit Fillets on Orange Fennel

1 fennel bulb, ½ lb carrots (about 8 oz), 1 small onion, 2 oranges,
¼ cup butter, 1 pinch sugar, Salt, Freshly ground black pepper,
1 cup vegetable stock, ½ cup herb crème fraîche, 1 small chile pepper,
1 tbs honey, 4 tbs olive oil, 1 lb rabbit fillets
Plus: Orange marmalade for garnish (optional)

Clean fennel bulb. Rinse fennel greens, pat dry, chop finely, and set aside. Cut bulb into quarters, remove core, and cut crosswise into strips. Clean carrots and, depending on their side, cut lengthwise into quarters or halves and crosswise into coarse pieces. Peel and mince onion. Peel oranges so that the white outer membrane is also removed and cut segments from between the inner membranes.

In a saucepan, heat butter and melt sugar. Stir in prepared vegetables and season with salt and pepper. Add stock and braise over medium heat for 10 minutes. Just before serving, stir in herb crème fraîche and orange segments.

Remove stem, seeds and interior from chile pepper, and mince. In a small bowl, combine chile pepper, honey and olive oil, and brush mixture onto the rabbit fillets. In a hot nonstick pan, fry meat on all sides for 5–7 minutes. Remove, season with salt and pepper, wrap in aluminum foil, and let stand for 5 minutes.

Spread orange-fennel mixture over the surface of 4 preheated plates. Remove rabbit fillets from the foil, cut on an angle into thin slices, arrange on the vegetables, and drizzle with the meat juice that accumulated on the foil. If desired, garnish with orange marmalade.

As a side dish, serve Spaghetti with Lemon Sauce (see recipe on page 31).

Jumbo Shrimp with Mandarin-Orange Papaya Sauce

8 peeled jumbo shrimp, Juice of 1 lime, 2 splashes Tabasco sauce,
½ tsp Worcestershire sauce, Salt, Freshly ground black pepper, 1 onion,
1 clove garlic, 1 ripe, sweet papaya, 4 mandarin oranges, 2 tbs butter,
1 tbs honey, 1 pinch cayenne pepper, ½ tsp turmeric,
1 dash sherry vinegar, 8 slices bacon
Plus: Toothpicks

Rinse shrimp under cold running water, slit down the backs, and remove veins. Pat slightly dry, place in a bowl, and mix with lime juice, Tabasco, Worcestershire sauce, salt, and pepper.

Peel and mince onion and garlic. Peel papaya, remove seeds, and cut into small pieces. Cut 2 mandarin oranges in half and squeeze out juice. Carefully peel the other 2 mandarin oranges and separate into segments. In a pan, heat half the butter and braise onion and garlic until translucent. Stir in papaya pieces, honey, cayenne, salt, and turmeric. Pour in mandarin orange juice and vinegar and simmer gently for another 5 minutes. Using a hand blender, purée sauce and add seasoning to taste.

Wrap 1 slice bacon around each jumbo shrimp and secure with a toothpick. In a pan, heat remaining butter and sauté shrimp on all sides for 3–4 minutes. Pour a pool of sauce onto 4 plates and place 2 shrimp on top of each. Garnish decoratively with mandarin orange segments.

Red Mullet on Mandarin-Orange Wild Rice

4 red mullet fillets (about 5 oz each), Juice of ½ lime,
Salt, Freshly cracked black pepper, 2 shallots, ⅓ cup olive oil,
1½ cups wild rice, 1 dash saffron threads, 3 cups vegetable stock,
4 mandarin oranges, 1 tbs chopped parsley

Rinse fish fillets, pat dry, and drizzle with lime juice. Season with salt and pepper. Peel and mince shallots. In a saucepan, heat half the olive oil and braise shallots until translucent. Sprinkle in wild rice, sauté for 1 minute while stirring, and season with saffron threads. Pour in stock, bring to a boil, cover, and cook rice over medium heat according to the package directions.

In the meantime, carefully peel mandarin oranges and separate into segments. As soon as the rice is done, heat remaining olive oil in a pan and braise fish fillets on both sides for 5 minutes. Lightly toss mandarin orange segments and parsley with the rice, distribute on plates, and arrange fish fillets on top.

 This recipe is also suitable for other types of fish, such as sole, redfish, and salmon.

DIPS AND SAUCES

Lemon-Scented Indian Spinach

1 lb fresh spinach, Salt, 2 lemons, 2 tbs ghee or clarified butter,
1 tsp black mustard seeds, 1 tsp cumin seeds,
½ tsp fenugreek seeds (health food or Asian market),
1¼ cups plain yogurt, 1 dash cayenne pepper

Sort spinach, rinse, and blanch in boiling, salted water. Remove, rinse under cold water, drain thoroughly, and chop finely. Peel lemons so that the white outer membrane is also removed and cut segments from between the inner membranes. In a pan, heat ghee and toast mustard seeds, cumin seeds, and fenugreek seeds while stirring constantly. Transfer to a bowl and let cool briefly. Lightly mix seeds with yogurt, lemon segments and spinach, and season to taste with cayenne and salt. Cover with plastic wrap and refrigerate for 1 hour. Serve with pieces of flatbread for dipping.

Ghee comes from Indian cuisine and consists of pure butter fat or clarified butter. You can either buy it pre-made in an Asian store or make it yourself: Simmer butter over medium heat for about 45 minutes. The browned parts of the butter will have settled to the bottom. To clarify the butter, pour it through a fine-mesh strainer lined with a cloth. The clarified butter will keep for 4 weeks.

Lemony Eggplant Spread

2 eggplants (about 1 lb), 2 cloves garlic, 1 shallot,
½ bunch Italian parsley, 2 lemons, 5 tbs olive oil,
1 tsp cumin seeds, Salt, Freshly ground black pepper
Plus: Finely chopped fruit of 1 lemon

Preheat oven to 400°F. Rinse eggplants, cut in half lengthwise, and pierce the skin several times with a fork. Place on a baking sheet with the cut sides down. Heat in the oven for 20 minutes until the skin forms blisters and appears shrunken. Remove from oven, let cool slightly, and peel.

In the meantime, peel garlic and shallot and chop somewhat coarsely. Rinse parsley, pat dry, and pluck leaves from stems. Squeeze juice from lemons. Using a blender or hand blender, finely purée eggplant with the other prepared ingredients. Pour purée into a bowl and sprinkle with chopped lemon.

 This eggplant purée makes an elegant dip, but can also serve as a savory side dish with grilled meat, especially lamb.

Avocado Cream

1 small chile pepper, 2 beefsteak tomatoes, 5 stalks cilantro,
2 ripe avocados, Juice of 1 lime, 1 cup sour cream,
Salt, Freshly ground black pepper

Remove stem, seeds, and interior from chile pepper and mince. Blanch beefsteak tomatoes, peel, remove cores and seeds, and dice finely. Rinse cilantro, pat dry, pluck leaves from stems, and chop finely.

Peel avocados, cut in half, remove pits, and chop coarsely. Using a blender or hand blender, finely purée avocados with lime juice and sour cream. Stir in chile pepper, tomatoes, and cilantro. Season with salt and pepper.

 Adding extremely fine lime pieces to the sauce adds to its refreshing flavor.

Red Bean Purée with Limes

8 oz cooked borlotti or pinto beans (canned), 1 onion, 2 cloves garlic,
5 tbs olive oil, 1 tbs tomato paste, Salt, Freshly ground black pepper,
1 tsp sugar, Juice of 2 limes, 1 cup vegetable stock, 1 tbs chopped cilantro

Pour beans into a colander and drain. Peel and mince onion and garlic.

In a pan, heat olive oil and briefly braise onion and garlic. Add beans and stir in tomato paste, salt, pepper, and sugar. Pour in lime juice and stock and simmer gently for 5 minutes.

Using a blender or hand blender, finely purée the contents of the pan. Pour into a bowl and sprinkle with cilantro.

 A thick layer of this extraordinary bean purée tastes phenomenal on flatbread or white bread.

Clementine Orange Dressing

5 clementine oranges, 2 sugar cubes, 1 lime,
4 tbs olive oil, 1 tbs maple syrup

Rinse clementine oranges, wipe dry, and rub sugar cubes onto the peels until they have fully absorbed the aroma. Squeeze juice from clementine oranges and lime and pour through a fine-mesh strainer. Lightly beat all ingredients together and refrigerate until needed.

 This dressing tastes fantastic on green salads, tomatoes, and avocados. It is also ideal for fruit salads.

Israeli Tahini Sauce

1 clove garlic, 1 large pinch salt, 4 lemons,
⅔ cup tahini (sesame paste, prepared product)

Peel garlic, squeeze through a press, and sprinkle with salt. Squeeze juice from lemons and pour juice through a strainer. In a small bowl, beat sesame paste and garlic until creamy. Pour into a gravy boat, cover with plastic wrap, and refrigerate until needed.

 How could there be falafel (little garbanzo bean balls) in pita bread without tahini sauce? This nutty-sweet-sour sauce tastes so good, try serving it with grilled dishes or just as a dip.

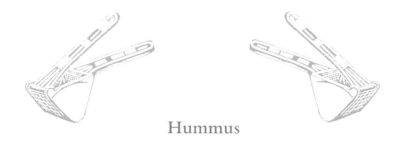

Hummus

2 lemons, 1 small onion, 2 cloves garlic, ½ bunch Italian parsley,
1 can cooked garbanzo beans (drained weight about 6 oz),
¼ cup olive oil, Salt, Freshly ground black pepper,
1 large pinch cayenne pepper, 1 large pinch chili powder,
½ tsp cumin seeds

Squeeze juice from lemons. Peel and mince onion and garlic. Rinse parsley, pat dry, and pluck leaves from stems. Pour garbanzo beans into a colander, rinse under cold water, and drain. Finely purée all ingredients using a blender or hand blender. Transfer to 4 individual bowls and serve.

 Serve this spicy spread with flatbread and salad.

Parsley Almond Sauce

½ bunch Italian parsley, 2 cloves garlic, Juice of 2 lemons,
1½ cups ground almonds, 1 tbs honey, ⅓ cup olive oil,
Salt, Freshly ground black pepper

Rinse parsley, pat dry, pluck leaves from stems, and chop finely. Peel garlic and dice somewhat coarsely. Finely purée all ingredients using a blender or hand blender. Season with salt and pepper and pour into a bowl.

Be sure to try this one! Use this sauce, for example, as a dip at your next fondue party.

Mandarin-Scented Banana Sauce

2 small bananas, Juice of 1 mandarin orange, Juice of 1 lime,
3 tbs mango chutney (prepared product), 1 cup sour cream,
Salt, Freshly ground black pepper, 1 pinch curry powder,
½ tsp sugar, 1 mandarin orange

Peel bananas, mash with a fork, and combine with mandarin orange juice and lemon juice. Gradually stir in all other ingredients except the mandarin orange. Season liberally to taste and transfer to a gravy boat. Carefully peel mandarin orange, separate into segments, and use to garnish sauce.

This banana sauce goes well with grilled meat, fish, and vegetables.

DESSERTS, CAKES, AND PASTRIES

Balsamic Strawberries with Lemon Cream

1 lb small strawberries, 2 tbs balsamic vinegar, 2 tbs sugar,
1¼ cups mascarpone cheese, 5 tbs heavy cream, 1 lime,
2 tbs powdered sugar, 2 tbs Limoncello (Italian lemon liqueur),
Several freshly chopped lemon balm leaves

Rinse strawberries, clean, pat dry with paper towels, and place in a wide bowl. Combine vinegar and sugar and drizzle over the strawberries. Cover the bowl with plastic wrap and let stand for about 1 hour at room temperature.

In the meantime, stir mascarpone with cream until smooth. Rinse lime under hot water, wipe dry, and grate off peel. Squeeze out juice. Add peel, juice, powdered sugar, and Limoncello to the cream. Transfer marinated strawberries to 4 shallow bowls and place a dollop of cream in the center of each. Garnish with chopped lemon balm.

 The success of this unusual recipe primarily depends on the quality of the ingredients. It's best if you use wild strawberries and aged balsamic vinegar.

Quick Mandarin Orange Dessert

1 egg, ½ cup sugar, 1¼ cups ricotta, ¾ cup plain yogurt,
3 tbs orange liqueur (e.g. Grand Marnier), ⅔ cup heavy cream,
2 large mandarin oranges

In a bowl, beat egg with sugar until foamy. Gradually stir in ricotta, yogurt, and 1 tbs orange liqueur. Whip cream and fold in. Carefully peel mandarin oranges, separate into segments, and lightly mix segments into the ricotta cream. Transfer to glass bowls. Just before serving, drizzle with orange liqueur.

Goes with ladyfingers, which can also serve as dessert spoons.

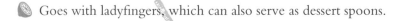

Whipped Orange Liqueur Cream

5 egg yolks, 5 tbs powdered sugar,
1 tbs orange liqueur (e.g. Grand Marnier),
Lemon balm leaves, Ladyfingers

In a saucepan, bring water to a boil. In a heat-resistant bowl that fits on top of the pan, beat egg yolks with powdered sugar. Place bowl on the hot double boiler and slowly pour in orange liqueur and 1–2 tbs water while beating the mixture constantly with a wire whisk. After 5–7 minutes, the mixture should have become a frothy cream. Remove bowl from double boiler, beat briefly over ice water, and immediately transfer to tall dessert glasses. Garnish with lemon balm leaves and serve with ladyfingers as dessert spoons.

You can also place several orange segments and a little orange juice in the dessert glasses and spoon the orange liqueur cream on top.

Berlin Air

1 pkg powdered fruit gelatin (about 1¾ oz), 4 eggs,
1 cup powdered sugar, Juice and grated peel of 1 lemon,
⅓ cup dry white wine, 1 pinch salt, 1½ cups raspberries

Soften gelatin in ¼ cup cold water. In the meantime, separate eggs. In a bowl, combine egg yolks, powdered sugar, lemon juice and lemon peel, and beat with a hand mixer until thick and creamy. In a small saucepan, heat white wine. Add softened gelatin and dissolve in wine while stirring, then stir this mixture into the egg yolk mixture. Beat egg whites with salt until stiff and carefully fold into mixture. Set aside in a cool place for about 1 hour. Before serving, rinse raspberries, pat dry, clean, and use to garnish cream.

 You can also garnish with ladyfingers.

Lemon Cream with Figs

2 tsp powdered gelatin, 4 eggs, ¾ cup sugar, 2 lemons,
4 fresh figs, Several fresh cilantro leaves

Soften gelatin in ¼ cup cold water. In the meantime, separate eggs. In a bowl, beat egg yolks with sugar until white and creamy. Squeeze juice from lemons. Dissolve wet gelatin in the microwave or in a saucepan over low heat. Carefully fold half the egg yolk mixture into the gelatin, stir in lemon juice and, finally, stir in remaining egg yolk mixture.

Beat egg whites until stiff and carefully fold into the cream. Rinse out 4 large, individual molds with cold water, pour in cream, and smooth out the surface. Refrigerate for about 3 hours.

Just before serving, rinse figs, remove stems, and cut each fig into 6 wedges. Run the tip of a knife around the edges of the molds to loosen cream and reverse onto 4 plates. Garnish around the edges with fig wedges and cilantro.

Candied Grapefruit with Red Mascarpone

2 pink grapefruits, 2 white grapefruits, ¾ cup sugar, 1 cup red wine,
2 blood oranges, ¾ cup mascarpone cheese

Peel 2 pink and 1 white grapefruit so that the white outer membrane is also removed, cut segments from between the inner membranes, and place in a bowl. Squeeze juice from fourth grapefruit. In a saucepan, combine juice, sugar, and red wine, bring to a boil and reduce over medium heat for 10–15 minutes until the mixture has a syrupy consistency. Pour syrup over grapefruit segments, cover bowl with plastic wrap, and refrigerate for about 2 hours.

In the meantime, peel 1 blood orange so that the white outer membrane is also removed and cut segments from between the inner membranes. Squeeze juice from second blood orange and stir juice into mascarpone until smooth.

Distribute candied grapefruit with the syrup in glass bowls, spoon mascarpone over the top, and garnish with blood orange segments.

Semolina Pudding with Citrus Fruit Sauce

For the semolina pudding:, 4½ cups buttermilk, ⅓ cup butter,
⅔ cup sugar, ½ tsp vanilla extract, ¾ cup semolina flour, 3 egg whites
For the fruit sauce: 3 mandarin oranges, 2 oranges, 1 tbs butter,
1 tbs sugar, 3 tbs apricot liqueur

For the semolina pudding: In a saucepan, combine buttermilk, butter and vanilla, and bring to a boil while stirring constantly. Sprinkle in sugar and semolina and quickly let boil down and thicken. Remove from heat and let cool briefly. Beat egg whites until stiff and fold into semolina pudding. Rinse out 4 glass bowls with cold water, fill with pudding, and refrigerate.

In the meantime, make the sauce: Peel mandarin oranges and separate into segments. Squeeze juice from oranges. In a pan, heat butter and melt sugar. Pour in orange juice, add mandarin orange segments, and flavor with apricot liqueur. Pour fruit sauce over the semolina pudding and serve.

Orange Gelatin with Vanilla Cream

1½ pkg powdered gelatin, 6 oranges, ½ cup sugar
Plus: 1½ cups blue grapes, 1 lime, 2 bananas, ¾ cup heavy cream,
2 tbs sugar, ½ tsp vanilla extract

Soften gelatin in ⅓ cup cold water. Rinse 1 orange under hot water and wipe dry. Using a zester, grate very fine zest from the peel. Squeeze juice from all the oranges and pour through a fine-mesh strainer. In a saucepan, heat a total of 2¼ cups orange juice (if necessary, add more juice to reach this amount) with sugar. Dissolve softened gelatin in orange juice while stirring. Rinse out 4 individual molds with cold water and pour in warm orange juice. Refrigerate for about 5 hours until firm.

Just before serving, rinse grapes and remove stems. Peel lime so that the white outer membrane is also removed and cut segments from between the inner membranes. Peel bananas, slice, and toss lightly with grapes and lime segments. Whip cream with sugar and vanilla until stiff.

Run the tip of a knife around the edges of the molds to loosen and unmold onto 4 plates. Arrange fruit around the edges and garnish each serving with a large dollop of vanilla cream.

 This dessert is also delicious if you use only mandarin oranges and grapefruit or grapefruit and oranges. It can serve, for example, as a "therapeutic" finale to a high-calorie meal.

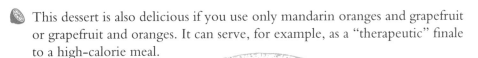

Iced Clementine Oranges

4 large clementine oranges, 1 tbs apricot jam, ¼ cup sugar
For the sorbet: ⅓ cup sugar, Juice of ½ lime or lemon,
2 tbs orange liqueur (e.g. Cointreau), ¾ cup heavy cream,
½ tsp vanilla extract

Rinse clementine oranges under hot water, wipe dry with paper towels, and cut a cap off each. Using a small sharp knife or grapefruit spoon (with a serrated tip), carefully remove fruit and set aside. Combine apricot jam and 2 tbs hot water and stir until smooth. Spread jam all over the outsides of the hollowed-out clementine peels. Shake sugar onto a flat plate, roll the clementine peels around in it to coat, and place in the freezer until needed.

In the meantime, make the sorbet: In a saucepan, combine sugar and 3 tbs water and bring to a boil. Remove from heat and let cool. Squeeze juice from clementine flesh and pour through a fine-mesh strainer. Stir clementine juice, lime or lemon juice, and orange liqueur into the sugar solution. Whip cream with vanilla until stiff and add to sugar solution.

Remove iced clementine shells from the freezer and fill with sorbet. Return to the freezer without the caps for another 30 minutes, then remove, place the caps on top, and return to the freezer for at least 2 hours.

 Serve in glass bowls or champagne saucers to give the clementines more stability. Let iced fruits thaw for about 10 minutes before serving and garnish with lemon balm leaves.

Blood Orange Parfait

2 egg yolks, Juice of ½ blood orange, ⅔ cup sugar,
1¼ cups heavy cream, 2 blood oranges, 1 tbs lemon balm strips,
1 tbs chopped pistachios

Using an electric hand mixer, beat egg yolks with orange juice and sugar until foamy. Whip cream until stiff and fold into egg yolk mixture. Rinse out a loaf pan with cold water, pour in the mixture, and smooth out the surface. Cover with plastic wrap, place in the freezer, and freeze for at least 3 hours.

About 20 minutes before serving, thaw parfait to room temperature. In the meantime, peel blood oranges so that the white outer membrane is also removed and cut segments from between the inner membranes.

Unmold the parfait, slice, and arrange on 4 dessert plates. Garnish with orange segments and sprinkle with lemon balm strips and pistachios.

 You can also prepare this parfait with other citrus fruits such as mandarin oranges, lemons, limes, or grapefruit.

Grapefruit Ice Cream

1 grapefruit, 1 cup ricotta, 2 tbs sugar, 2 tbs maple syrup,
½ cup crème fraîche, ¾ cup heavy cream
Plus: Segments of 1 pink grapefruit

Squeeze juice from grapefruit and pour through a fine-mesh strainer. In a bowl, combine grapefruit juice, ricotta, sugar, maple syrup, and crème fraîche. Whip cream until stiff and fold in.

Now either prepare the ricotta in an ice cream maker or, if you don't have one, proceed as follows: Cut 2 additional grapefruits in half, hollow out, and fill halves with ricotta ice cream. Place in the freezer and freeze for at least 2 hours. Thaw ice cream for 10 minutes before serving and garnish with grapefruit segments.

 Goes with crushed pralines, ice cream wafer cookies, and a small glass of orange liqueur.

Crêpes Suzette

1¼ cups flour, ½ cup powdered sugar, 1 egg, 2 egg yolks,
Grated peel from ½ lemon, ⅔ cup milk, ⅓ cup heavy cream,
⅓ cup butter, 2 oranges, 2 lemons, ⅓ cup sugar,
3 tbs orange liqueur (e.g. Grand Marnier), 3 tbs brandy
Plus: Powdered sugar for decoration

Using an electric hand mixer, beat flour, powdered sugar, egg, egg yolks, lemon peel, milk, and cream into a runny batter and let stand for about 15 minutes. In a wide pan, heat a little butter. One at a time, cook thin, golden crêpes, adding more butter each time. Stack crêpes on a plate and cover with aluminum foil.

Rinse oranges and lemons under hot water and wipe dry with paper towels. Remove only the thinnest possible zest from the fruits. Squeeze juice from fruits and pour through a fine-mesh strainer.

In a deep pan or wok, heat 1 tbs butter and melt sugar while stirring. Stir in zest, juice, and orange liqueur. Fold or roll up crêpes and place in the liquid. Pour brandy into a ladle, heat over a lighter or gas flame, light, and pour over the crêpes. Distribute on 4 plates and dust with powdered sugar.

 Naturally, you can also make the crêpes right at the table with a special crêpe maker. This always impresses your guests.

Chocolate Fruit Fondue

For the fondue:, 6–7 oz milk chocolate, ⅓ cup heavy cream
For dipping: 1 cup strawberries (almost 8 oz), 2 oranges,
1 sweet pink grapefruit, 2 mandarin oranges,
1 baby pineapple, 2 bananas
Plus: 4 fondue forks

Rinse and clean strawberries. Peel oranges and grapefruit so that the white outer membrane is also removed and cut segments from between the inner membranes. Carefully peel mandarin oranges and separate into segments. Peel baby pineapple, cut in half, remove core, and cut into bite-sized pieces. Peel bananas and slice. Arrange all ingredients in small bowls and place on the table.

For the fondue: Break up chocolate into small pieces and place in a heat-resistant bowl with cream. Melt either in the microwave or over a hot double boiler. Mix well with the cream, pour into a fondue pot or earthenware vessel, and keep warm on a table-top alcohol burner. Pierce fruits with fondue forks as desired, dip into the chocolate, and enjoy.

 If you don't have a suitable vessel, you can also pour the chocolate into individual bowls.

Warm Fruit Salad in Orange Halves

3 large oranges, 1 small mango, 8 lychees, 1 banana, 1 tbs butter,
1 tbs powdered sugar, 2 tbs cream sherry, ½ cup chopped walnuts,
4 scoops mandarin orange ice cream or lemon sorbet (optional)

Rinse oranges, wipe dry, and cut in half. Even off the bottoms of the halves of 2 oranges so they won't easily tip over. Remove fruit and dice finely. Squeeze juice from the third orange. Peel mango and cut into thin wedges around the pit. Peel lychees, remove pits, and cut into strips. Peel and slice banana.

In a pan, heat butter and stir in powdered sugar. Drizzle with orange juice and cream sherry. Add prepared fruits, stir around briefly, and pour contents of the pan into the orange halves. Garnish with chopped walnuts and, if desired, place 1 scoop of mandarin orange ice cream or lemon sorbet next to or on top of the fruit salad.

 You can change the combination of fruit to match the season. Salad is also delicious in grapefruit halves.

French Orange Soufflés

Makes 4–5 ramekins

1 orange, 4 eggs, 7 tbs flour, 1¼ cups milk,
1 tbs butter, ½ cup sugar, 2 tbs orange liqueur (e.g. Grand Marnier)
Plus: Butter and sugar for the ramekins, Powdered sugar for decoration

Rinse orange, wipe dry, and grate off very fine zest with a zester. Cut orange in half, squeeze out juice, and pour through a fine-mesh strainer. Butter 4 individual ramekins and sprinkle with sugar. Separate eggs. Beat egg whites until stiff and refrigerate until needed.

In a saucepan, combine flour and milk. Heat and reduce while stirring constantly. Remove from heat and let the mixture cool.

Preheat oven to 400°F. Whisk together egg yolks, sugar, orange liqueur, orange juice and orange zest, and stir into cooled milk mixture. Finally, fold in egg whites. Fill ramekins to within ¼ inch of the top. Place on a baking sheet and bake in the oven for about 15 minutes until golden brown. Remove, dust with powdered sugar and serve immediately.

Soufflés behave like primadonnas. Rather than wait for the guests, the guests must wait for them. You won't want to miss the moment when they are all puffed up—in no time at all, they'll collapse again.

Orange Spritz Cookies

For the dough: ¾ cup softened butter, ½ cup sugar, 4 egg yolks,
⅓ cup finely diced almond paste, Juice of ½ orange, 2 cups flour
For the glaze: 3 tbs orange marmalade, 6–7 oz dark chocolate glaze

In a bowl, combine butter, sugar and egg yolks, and beat with an electric hand mixer until thick and creamy. Gradually add remaining batter ingredients.

Preheat oven to 400°F. Spoon soft dough into a pastry bag with a star tip and pipe strips 2- to 3-inches long onto a baking sheet lined with parchment paper. Bake strips in the oven for about 12 minutes until golden.

Remove and let cool briefly. Spread the bottoms of half the cookies with orange marmalade and sandwich together with the remaining cookies. Then coat half or all of each cookie sandwich with melted chocolate glaze.

You can also make this recipe with mandarin oranges or limes instead of oranges. If you don't want chocolate glaze, leave it off and dust the cookies with powdered sugar.

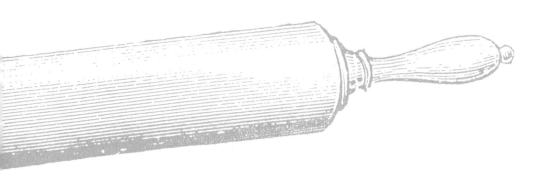

Orange Kisses

For the dough:, 1⅔ cups flour, ⅓ cup cornstarch,
1½ tsp baking powder, ½ cup sugar, ¾ cup butter, 1 egg,
A little grated peel of lemon
For the topping: 1 generous cup ground almonds, ⅓ cup sugar,
Juice and grated peel of 1 orange
For the glaze: 1 cup powdered sugar, Juice of ½ orange
Plus: Flour for the work surface

In a bowl, quickly mix together all the dough ingredients and process into a smooth pastry dough. Shape into a ball, wrap in plastic wrap, and refrigerate for 1 hour.

Preheat oven to 400°F. Knead dough thoroughly on a floured work surface and divide in half. Roll out each half to a thickness of about ¼ inch and cut out circles with about a 1½-inch diameter.

For the topping: Combine almonds, sugar, orange juice and orange peel, and mix thoroughly. Place about ¼ tsp of the almond mixture in the center of each dough circle and fold up the edges slightly. Place orange kisses on a baking sheet lined with parchment paper and bake in the oven for 15–20 minutes until golden brown. Cool briefly on a cooling rack. In the meantime, combine orange juice and powdered sugar, stir until smooth, and spread onto the cookies.

Lemon Cookies with Pistachios

For the dough:, 2½ cups flour, 2 cups powdered sugar,
Juice and grated peel of 1 lemon,
½ cup finely chopped candied lemon peel, 2 eggs, ⅔ cup butter
For the frosting: 2½ cups powdered sugar,
Juice and grated peel of 1 lemon
Plus: Flour for the work surface, About ⅓ cup apricot jam,
½ cup finely chopped pistachios

In a bowl, combine flour and powdered sugar and make a well in the center. Stir in lemon juice, lemon peel, candied lemon peel, eggs and butter cut into bits, and knead into a smooth dough. Shape into a ball, wrap in plastic wrap, and refrigerate for 1 hour.

Knead dough thoroughly on a floured work surface and divide into thirds. Roll out each third one at a time to a thickness of about ¼ inch and cut into cookies of any shape (e.g., stars, diamonds, circles).

Preheat oven to 400°F. Place cookie shapes on a baking sheet lined with parchment paper and bake for about 10 minutes until golden brown. Remove, spread the bottoms of half the cookies with apricot jam, and sandwich together with the remaining cookies.

For the frosting, combine powdered sugar, lemon juice, and lemon peel, stir until smooth and use to coat cookies. Sprinkle with pistachios.

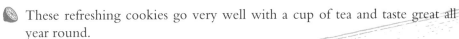 These refreshing cookies go very well with a cup of tea and taste great all year round.

Lemon Cake

Makes 1 loaf pan (about 12-inches long)
4 eggs, 2½ cups powdered sugar, 2 tbs rum, Grated peel of ½ lemon,
1 cup butter, 1 cup flour, 1 cup cornstarch, 1 tsp baking powder, 2 lemons
For the frosting: 2 cups powdered sugar, 4 tbs lemon juice
Plus: Butter for the pan, 1 wooden toothpick

Preheat oven to 350°F (or slightly higher). Butter the pan. In a bowl, beat eggs and powdered sugar with a hand mixer to form a light, creamy mixture. Add rum and lemon peel. In a saucepan, melt butter and let cool until lukewarm.

In the meantime, in a second bowl combine flour, cornstarch and baking powder, and sift through a fine-mesh strainer. Carefully stir flour mixture and butter into the egg-sugar mixture one spoonful at a time. Pour batter into the pan and smooth out the surface. Bake in the oven for 1–1¼ hours until golden brown (do the toothpick test!). Remove, let stand briefly, reverse onto a cooling rack, and let cool until lukewarm.

Pierce cake at regularly spaced intervals with a toothpick. Squeeze juice from lemons and pour through a fine-mesh strainer. Drizzle juice one spoonful at a time into the holes made by the toothpick in order to drench the cake.

For the frosting: Sift powdered sugar into a bowl and gradually stir in lemon juice. Coat cake with the frosting and let cool completely before serving.

 This cake is especially pretty if you decorate it with lemon zest in addition to the lemon frosting.

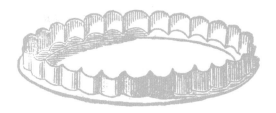

Lemon Tart

Makes 1 tart pan (12-inch diameter)
For the dough: 1⅔ cups flour, ⅓ cup sugar, ½ tsp vanilla extract,
Grated peel of 1 lemon, ⅓ cup cold butter, 1 egg yolk
For the topping: 2–3 lemons, 4 eggs, 1 egg yolk,
1 cup sugar, 1 cup heavy cream, 1 tbs powdered sugar
Plus: Butter for the pan, Dried beans for blind baking,
Powdered sugar for decoration

For the dough: On a work surface, mix flour, sugar, vanilla, and lemon peel. Cut butter into bits and add butter and egg yolk to flour mixture. Quickly knead ingredients into a smooth dough. Shape into a ball, wrap in plastic wrap, and refrigerate for 30 minutes.

Preheat oven to 350°F. Roll out dough to fit the greased tart pan. Line the pan with the dough, forming an edge 1-inch high. Pierce dough several times with a fork. Cut out a piece of parchment paper to fit the pan and place on the dough. Add enough beans so that the bottom of the pan is well covered and bake blind for 10 minutes. Remove from oven and remove beans and parchment paper. Reduce oven temperature to 300°F.

In the meantime, make the topping: Rinse lemons under hot water, dry thoroughly, and grate off peel. Squeeze out juice. In a bowl, beat eggs, egg yolk, and sugar until foamy. Stir in lemon peel and juice. Whip cream until stiff and fold in carefully. Pour mixture into the pre-baked shell and smooth out the surface. Return tart to the oven and bake for about 50 minutes until lightly browned. Let cool. Before serving, sift powdered sugar on top.

Glazed Lemon Cream Cake

Makes 1 springform pan (10-inch diameter)
For the pastry shell: ¼ cup sugar, 2 tbs hot water, 2½ cups flour,
½ cup softened butter (1 stick), 1 cup powdered sugar,
1 egg, Grated peel of 1 lemon, 1 pinch salt
For the filling: 1 pkg powdered gelatin, 1 cup sugar,
⅔ cup butter, Juice and grated peel of 2 lemons,
2 tbs hot water, 3 eggs
Plus: Butter for the pan, Flour for processing,
Dried beans for blind baking, 2 tbs sugar

For the dough: Combine sugar, hot water, flour, butter, powdered sugar, egg, lemon peel and salt, and knead thoroughly on a work surface. Shape into a ball, wrap in plastic wrap, and refrigerate for 30 minutes.

Butter the springform pan. Preheat oven to 400°F. Once again, knead dough thoroughly on a floured work surface and roll it out to fit the springform pan. Line the pan with the dough, forming an edge 1- to 1½-inches high. Pierce dough several times with a fork. Cut out a piece of parchment paper to fit the pan, place on the dough, sprinkle with dried beans, and bake blind in the oven for 25–30 minutes. Remove from oven and remove beans and parchment paper. Let cool completely.

For the topping: Soften gelatin in ¼ cup cold water for 10 minutes. In a heat-resistant bowl, combine sugar, butter, lemon juice, lemon peel and hot water, and beat over a hot double boiler until foamy. Stir softened gelatin into the warm mixture and dissolve. Stir in eggs. Remove bowl from double boiler and beat over ice water.

Pour cooled cream into the pastry shell and smooth out the surface. Refrigerate for at least 2 hours so the cream can set completely. In a saucepan, heat 2 tbs water with 2 tbs sugar and reduce to a syrup. Let cool and use to glaze the cake.

You can also peel 1 lemon, cut it up into small pieces, garnish the cake with it, and then drizzle on the sugar solution.

Limoncino Coffee Ring

Makes 1 bundt pan
3⅓ cups flour, 3 tsp baking powder, 1½ cups softened butter (3 sticks),
2 ¼ cups sugar, 1 tsp vanilla extract, 8 eggs
Plus: Butter and flour for the pan, ¾ cup sugar, ¾ cup Limoncino
(Italian lemon liqueur), Powdered sugar for decoration

Preheat oven to 400°F. Butter and flour bundt pan. Using an electric hand mixer, process flour, baking powder, butter, sugar, vanilla, and eggs into a batter. Pour into pan and smooth out the surface. Bake in the oven on the bottom rack for 60–65 minutes until golden brown. Remove, run the tip of a knife around the edges to loosen slightly, and let cool in the pan.

In the meantime, combine sugar and 1 cup water in a saucepan, bring to a boil, and reduce for about 5 minutes while stirring until mixture has a syrupy consistency. Remove from heat. Let syrup cool slightly and then stir in lemon liqueur.

Spoon mixture onto the cake in the pan to drench and let stand so it can soak in well. Then unmold and dust with a thick layer of powdered sugar.

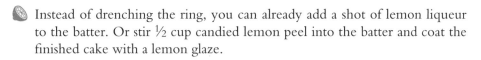 Instead of drenching the ring, you can already add a shot of lemon liqueur to the batter. Or stir ½ cup candied lemon peel into the batter and coat the finished cake with a lemon glaze.

Multivitamin Cake

Makes 1 bundt pan
¾ cup softened butter, 1 cup, plus 2 tbs sugar, 4 eggs,
½ tsp vanilla extract, 3 tsp baking powder,
1 tsp unsweetened cocoa powder,
⅓ cup mixed fruit juice (e.g., carrot, apple),
Juice of 1 orange, 2 cups flour
For the frosting: 2 cups powdered sugar, Juice of 1 lime
Plus: Butter and flour for the pan

Preheat oven to 400°F. Butter and flour bundt pan. In a bowl, gradually combine all the batter ingredients and process into a smooth batter. Pour into the pan and smooth out the surface.

Bake cake in the oven for about 45 minutes until golden brown. Remove, let cool briefly, and reverse out of the pan. Combine powdered sugar and lime juice, stir until smooth, and spread over the cake.

 I bake this delicious cake at least once a month for my son Philipp. He's a little gourmand!

Fruit Cheese Cake with Limes

Makes 1 springform pan (10–12 inch)
4 eggs, 1 cup softened butter (2 sticks), 1 cup sugar, 1 lb cream cheese,
½ tsp vanilla extract, 3 tsp baking powder, 1 pkg vanilla pudding mix,
⅓ cup semolina, Juice of 1 lime, ½ lime, finely chopped
Plus: Butter for the pan, Powdered sugar for decoration

Preheat oven to 300°F. Butter springform pan. Separate eggs. Using an electric hand mixer, beat butter, sugar, and egg yolks until thick and creamy. Gradually stir in remaining ingredients. Finally, beat egg whites until stiff and fold in. Pour batter into the pan and smooth out the surface.

Bake in the oven for 55–60 minutes until golden brown. Remove, let cool, and remove ring from pan. Dust cooled cake with powdered sugar.

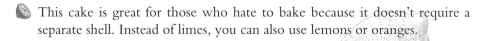 This cake is great for those who hate to bake because it doesn't require a separate shell. Instead of limes, you can also use lemons or oranges.

Orange Carrot Cake

Makes 1 springform pan (12 inch)
12 slices zwieback, ½ lb carrots, 1 tbs honey,
Juice and grated peel of 1 orange, Juice of ½ lemon, 5 eggs,
4 tbs hot water, 1 cup sugar, 2¼ cups ground hazelnuts
Plus: Butter and flour for the pan, Segments of 1 orange,
2 cups powdered sugar

Preheat oven to 350°F. Butter and flour a springform pan. Finely grate zwieback. Clean carrots and grate finely. In a bowl, combine zwieback crumbs, grated carrots, honey, orange juice, orange peel, and lemon juice.

Separate eggs. Beat egg yolks with hot water and sugar until thick and creamy. Stir in hazelnuts and carrot mixture. Beat egg whites until stiff and fold in.

Pour batter into the pan and bake in the oven for up to 60 minutes. Remove and let cool.

In the meantime, peel orange so that the white outer membrane is also removed and cut segments from between the inner membranes. Drain well and combine the juice that escapes with powdered sugar. Stir until smooth and use to glaze cake. Decoratively arrange orange segments on top as garnish and glaze them as well.

This cake is best if you serve it right when it's done cooling.

MARMALADES, JELLIES, AND CHUTNEYS

Orange Jelly

10 oranges (navel), Juice of 1 lemon, if needed, 4 cups sugar,
1 pkg powdered fruit pectin (about 1¾ oz), ⅛ tsp baking soda

Rinse oranges under hot water and wipe dry. Using a zester, remove long strips of peel lengthwise down the oranges and set aside. Cut oranges in half and squeeze out juice. Measure out 3 cups juice, supplementing with lemon juice and a little water if necessary. Pour juice into a large pot. Stir sugar, pectin, baking soda, and zest into juice. Heat mixture and boil hard for 2 minutes, stirring constantly (note: the liquid forms some foam). Immediately pour jelly into hot, sterilized jelly jars, seal tightly immediately, and stand upside-down for several minutes.

 This orange jelly isn't bitter like English orange marmalade, but is sweet and fruity.

Lemon Apple Jelly

2¼ cups freshly squeezed lemon juice, 2¼ cups apple juice,
4 cups sugar, 1 pkg powdered fruit pectin (about 1¾ oz),
Several stalks fresh lemon balm

In a bowl, combine lemon juice, apple juice, sugar, and pectin powder. Cover with plastic wrap and refrigerate for at least 1 hour. In the meantime, rinse lemon balm, pat dry, pluck leaves from stalks, and cut into strips.

Pour fruit mixture into a wide, shallow pot and bring to a boil. Boil hard for 1 minute while stirring constantly. Remove from heat and stir in lemon balm. Immediately pour jelly into hot, sterilized jelly jars and seal tightly.

Tomato Orange Marmalade

1 lb small ripe tomatoes, 2 oranges, 2½ cups sugar,
1 pkg powdered fruit pectin (about 1¾ oz),
2 tbs pickled green peppercorns,
2 tbs orange liqueur (e.g., Grand Marnier)

Blanch tomatoes and peel. Rinse oranges and wipe dry. Using a zester, remove paper-thin zest from 1 orange peel and then cut orange in half and squeeze out juice. Peel second orange so that the white outer membrane is also removed, cut segments from between the inner membranes, and cut into equally-sized pieces.

In a saucepan, combine 2¼ cups water, sugar, pectin and orange juice, and bring to a boil while stirring. Add tomatoes and orange pieces and simmer gently for 5 minutes while stirring carefully. Use a skimmer to remove any foam that forms on the surface.

Finally, stir peppercorns and orange peel into the contents of the saucepan. Remove from heat and pour immediately into hot, sterilized jelly jars. Rinse out jar lids with orange liqueur (pour from lid to lid) and screw tightly onto the jars.

🍊 This fruit-and-vegetable marmalade tastes fantastic on white or whole-wheat bread.

🍊 For almost all the marmalade and jelly recipes, I say to rinse out the lids with alcohol. On the one hand, it gives off a wonderful fragrance when you first open the jars. On the other hand, the alcohol works as a disinfectant so that the marmalade keeps longer.

Carrot Marmalade with Oranges and Lemons

1 lb carrots, 3 oranges, 3 lemons, 2⅔ cups sugar,
1 pkg powdered fruit pectin (about 1¾ oz),
2 tbs orange liqueur (e.g., Grand Marnier)

Clean carrots and grate most of them very finely using a food processor or a grater. Using a sharp knife, cut remaining carrots into matchsticks.

Rinse oranges and lemons under hot water and wipe thoroughly dry. Cut a spiral strip of peel from 1 orange and 1 lemon that is so thin that the white membrane remains on the fruit. Cut peels into pieces the same size as the carrot strips. Squeeze juice from all oranges and lemons.

In a saucepan, combine all prepared ingredients, including orange and lemon juice, with the sugar and pectin powder and bring to a boil. Boil hard for 5 minutes while stirring constantly. Remove from heat and pour immediately into hot, sterilized jelly jars. Rinse out jar lids with orange liqueur (pour from lid to lid) and screw tightly onto the jars.

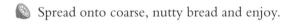 Spread onto coarse, nutty bread and enjoy.

Lemon Orange Marmalade with Ginger

1 lb lemons, 1 lb oranges, 1½-inch chunk fresh ginger root,
⅓ cup candied orange and lemon peel, mixed, 4 cups sugar,
1 pkg powdered fruit pectin (about 1¾ oz), 2 tbs brandy

Rinse lemons and oranges under hot water and wipe thoroughly dry. Using a zester, grate off very fine zest. Peel all fruit, place in a food processor, and purée either coarsely or finely, depending on the consistency you want. Peel ginger and grate finely.

In a saucepan, combine all ingredients except the brandy and bring to a boil. Boil hard for 5 minutes while stirring constantly. Remove from heat and pour immediately into hot, sterilized jelly jars. Rinse out jar lids with brandy (pour from lid to lid) and screw tightly onto the jars.

 This recipe will particularly appeal to fans of English marmalade. Naturally, you can also rinse out the jar lids with gin or whiskey.

Grapefruit Marmalade with Mandarin Oranges

1 pomelo, 1 lb pink grapefruits, 1 lb mandarin oranges,
4 cups sugar, 1 pkg powdered fruit pectin (about 1¾ oz),
2 tbs Limoncello (Italian lemon liqueur)

Rinse pomelo, wipe thoroughly dry, and peel. Place peel in boiling hot water and simmer gently for about 10 minutes. Remove and chop finely.

In the meantime, peel 1 grapefruit so that the white outer membrane is also removed and cut segments from between the inner membranes. Then cut segments into smaller pieces. Squeeze juice from remaining citrus fruits.

In a saucepan, combine all prepared ingredients, including lemon juice, with the sugar and gelling powder. Heat while stirring constantly and boil for 4–5 minutes.

Remove from heat and pour immediately into hot, sterilized jelly jars. Rinse out jar lids with Limoncello (pour from lid to lid) and screw tightly onto the jars.

Grapefruit Banana Preserves with Walnuts

1 lb pink grapefruits, 1 lb bananas,
4 cups sugar, 1 pkg powdered fruit pectin (about 1¾ oz),
1 cup chopped walnuts, 2 tbs banana liqueur

Peel half the grapefruits so that the white outer membrane is also removed. Cut segments from between the inner membranes and chop finely. Squeeze juice from remaining grapefruits. Peel bananas, cut lengthwise into quarters, and crosswise into pieces.

In a saucepan, combine all prepared ingredients, sugar and gelling powder, and bring to a boil. Boil hard for 5 minutes while stirring constantly. Remove from heat, stir in walnuts, and pour immediately into hot, sterilized jelly jars. Rinse out jar lids with banana liqueur (pour from lid to lid) and screw tightly onto the jars.

Pineapple Grapefruit Preserves with Rum Raisins

¾ cup raisins, 2 tbs white rum (e.g., Bacardi),
1 lb pineapple (peeled and cored), 1 lb pink grapefruits,
4 cups sugar, 1 pkg powdered fruit pectin (about 1¾ oz)

In a small bowl, pour rum over raisins. Chop pineapple very finely. Peel grapefruits so that the white outer membrane is also removed, cut segments from between the inner membranes, and chop finely. In a bowl, combine rum raisins and prepared fruits, cover with plastic wrap, and refrigerate for 1 hour.

In a saucepan, combine fruit mixture, sugar and pectin, and bring to a boil. Boil hard for about 4 minutes while stirring constantly. Remove from heat, pour immediately into hot, sterilized jelly jars, and seal tightly.

You simply must try this jam on a piece of pound cake.

Arabian Lemon Chutney

1 large onion, 2 small red chile peppers, 5 large lemons,
3 tbs vegetable oil, ½ cup brown sugar, ½ cup dry white wine,
1 pinch salt, 1 tsp crushed peppercorns, ¼ tsp cumin

Peel onion and chop finely. Remove stems, seeds and interiors from chile peppers, and mince. Rinse lemons and wipe dry. Using a zester, remove zest from peels and chop finely. Remove white membranes from lemons and cut fruit into small pieces, removing any seeds.

In a saucepan, heat vegetable oil and braise onion and chile peppers. Stir in lemon peel, lemon, sugar, and white wine. Season with salt, pepper, and cumin.

Simmer gently over medium heat for about 15 minutes while stirring constantly. Pour into a jar or bowl, let cool, and store covered in the refrigerator.

 This sweet-and-sour, savory chutney tastes great with grilled dishes. It keeps in the refrigerator for at least 1 week.

BEVERAGES

Brazilian Caipirinha

Makes 1 tall glass
1 lime, 1 tsp brown cane sugar,
3 tbs Cachaça (Brazilian sugarcane brandy), 4 tbs crushed ice

Rinse lime, wipe dry, and cut up peel coarsely. Place in the bottom of a glass, sprinkle with sugar, and crush and squeeze with a wooden spoon. Add Cachaça and crushed ice and stir.

Mexican Margarita

Makes 1 cocktail glass
Juice of ½ lemon, 3 tbs tequila,
1 tbs orange liqueur (e.g., Cointreau), 2 ice cubes
For garnish: Juice of 1½ lemons, 1 tbs salt

For the garnish: Pour lemon juice and salt onto 2 separate plates. First dip the rim of the cocktail glass into lemon juice and then rotate it in the salt. Briefly place glass in the freezer so the coating won't run.

In a cocktail shaker, combine lemon juice, tequila, orange liqueur and ice cubes, and shake vigorously. Pour into the glass and serve immediately.

You can also use limes instead of lemons. It won't taste the same as the original recipe but it will have an interesting tanginess.

Mexican Tequila Sunrise

Makes 1 highball glass
1 shot tequila, ½ cup orange juice, 5 ice cubes, 1 tbs grenadine syrup
Plus: Pineapple chunks, Fresh mint leaves

In a cocktail shaker, combine tequila, orange juice and ice cubes, and shake well. Drizzle grenadine syrup into the glass and pour in cocktail through a bar or fine-mesh strainer. Garnish with pineapple and mint.

Chilean Pisco Sour

Makes 4 shot glasses
1 tbs sugar, Juice of 1½ lemons,
3 tbs pisco (Chilean brandy, may substitute European), 3 ice cubes
For garnish: Juice of ½ lemon, 2 tbs sugar

For the garnish: Pour lemon juice and sugar onto 2 separate plates. First dip the rims of the shot glasses into lemon juice and then rotate in the sugar. Place the 4 glasses in the freezer for 30 minutes.

In a cocktail shaker, combine sugar, lemon juice, pisco and ice cubes, and shake vigorously. Remove glasses from the freezer and strain pisco through a bar or fine-mesh strainer.

Exotic Blue Ocean

Makes 1 highball glass
1 grapefruit, 1 shot tequila, ½ shot blue Curaçao,
½ shot passion fruit syrup, 4 ice cubes, Ice-cold Sprite to top off

Rinse grapefruit and cut in half. For the garnish, cut 1 slice and set aside. Squeeze out juice and pour through a bar or fine-mesh strainer. In a cocktail shaker, mix tequila, blue Curaçao, passion fruit syrup, and ice cubes. Pour into a highball glass and top up with Sprite. Garnish glass with the grapefruit slice.

Gin Fizz

Makes 1 tall glass
4 ice cubes, 1½ shots gin, Juice of ½ lemon,
1 tbs sugar syrup, About ½ cup cold club soda
For garnish: 1 slice lemon

In a cocktail shaker, combine ice cubes, gin, lemon juice and syrup, and shake until the ice cubes are well crushed. Pour into a glass and top up with club soda. Garnish glass with the lemon slice.

Grapefruit Fizz

Makes 1 highball glass
Juice of 1 pink grapefruit, Juice of 1 mandarin orange, Juice of 1 lime,
1½ shots white rum, 1 shot sugar syrup, 3 tbs crushed ice
For garnish: 2 slices pink grapefruit

Pour grapefruit, mandarin orange, and lime juice through a bar or fine-mesh strainer. In a cocktail shaker, mix all ingredients and pour into the glass. Garnish glass with the grapefruit slices.

Thai Siam

Makes 1 highball glass
½ banana, Juice of ½ lime, Juice of 2-3 oranges,
1 (scant) shot coconut syrup, 2 tbs crushed ice
For garnish: 2 cape gooseberries

Peel banana, chop coarsely, and purée in a blender with all the other ingredients until smooth. Pour into the glass and garnish with cape gooseberries.

Orange Fruit Punch

Makes 1 punch bowl (about 3½ qt)
2¼ cups black tea, 2¼ cups fruit tea, 2¼ cups red wine,
1 cup mixed fruit juice, 1 cup sugar, 1 cinnamon stick, 2 whole cloves,
2 star anise, 1 bourbon vanilla bean, 2 oranges, 2 lemons

In a wide pot, combine both teas, red wine, fruit juice and sugar, and mix thoroughly. Add cinnamon, cloves, and anise. Slit open vanilla bean lengthwise and add. Slowly heat mixture.

In the meantime, rinse oranges and lemons under hot water and dry thoroughly with a cloth. Grate off a fine layer of peel and stir into the pot. Cut fruits in half, squeeze out juice, and pour through a fine-mesh strainer into the pot. As soon as the punch starts to boil, remove from heat and let stand for another 5 minutes. Remove spices and season to taste.

You can also vary the punch with mandarin orange juice. If children are drinking with you, you can replace the red wine with the same amount of fruit tea.

Planter's Punch

Makes 1 highball glass
1 shot white rum, 1 shot brown rum, Juice of 1 orange,
Juice of ¼ lemon, ¼ cup pineapple juice, ½ shot grenadine, 12 ice cubes
For garnish: 1 slice pineapple, 2 maraschino cherries, 1 toothpick

In a cocktail shaker, combine all ingredients except 4 ice cubes and shake vigorously. Place remaining ice cubes in a highball glass and pour drink through a bar or fine-mesh strainer into the glass. Garnish glass with the pineapple slice. Pierce maraschino cherries with the toothpick and serve with the drink.

Old-Fashioned "Cold Duck" Punch

Makes 1 punch bowl (about 3½ qt)
1 lemon, 10 ice cubes, 6¾ cups chilled, semisweet, white Mosel wine,
1 bottle ice-cold sparkling wine

Rinse lemons and wipe thoroughly dry. Using a sharp knife, cut off a spiral strip of peel so that the white membrane remains on the fruit.

About 30 minutes before serving, place ice cubes in the bottom of the punch bowl, place lemon peel on top, and add white wine. Let stand. Finally, add sparkling wine, remove lemon peel, and ladle punch into glasses.

 This is the traditional way to prepare this punch. Today in the age of the dry white wine, you can also prepare it with a White Burgundy, Edelzwicker, or Green Veltliner and use Prosecco.

Hot Sangria

Makes 4 heat-resistant mugs
3¼ cups Spanish red wine, 1 tsp sugar, 1 orange,
1 lemon, 1 cinnamon stick
For garnish: 1 mandarin orange, 1 banana

In a saucepan, combine red wine and sugar, stir, and bring to a boil. In the meantime, rinse orange and lemon and wipe thoroughly dry. Using a sharp knife, cut off a spiral strip of peel so that the white membrane remains on the fruit. Slice orange and lemon and add to red wine along with cinnamon stick. Simmer gently over low heat for 5 minutes.

For garnish: Peel mandarin orange and banana, cut both into small pieces, and distribute in the mugs. Pour hot sangria over the top, remove cinnamon stick, and serve with lemon spirals as garnish.

Winter Vitamin Drink

Makes 4 glasses
2 pink grapefruits, 1 banana,
About 2¾ cups frozen raspberries, thawed, 1 cup buttermilk

Peel grapefruits and banana and cut into small pieces. In a blender, purée all ingredients and pour into 4 glasses.

Ice-Cold Citrus Mix

Makes 4 tall glasses
4 pink grapefruits, 4 mandarin oranges, 1 lemon, 2 oranges
For garnish: 2 tbs sugar, ½ lemon, About 16 ice cubes, 1 tbs honey

For garnish: Pour sugar onto a plate. Rub lemon half around the rims of the glasses, rotate rims in the sugar, and place glasses in the freezer for 15 minutes.

In the meantime, squeeze juice from citrus fruits. Remove glasses from freezer. Place 4 ice cubes in each glass and top with a dollop of honey. Pour citrus juices through a bar or fine-mesh strainer into the glasses.

🍋 You can also garnish with fresh fruits or lemon balm leaves.

Lime Tomato Juice

Makes 4 tall glasses
Juice of 2 limes, 3 cups tomato juice, 2 tbs ketchup,
10 ice cubes, Salt, Freshly ground black pepper
For garnish: 4 cherry tomatoes, 4 orange wedges,
4 cocktail or bamboo skewers

In a blender, blend lime juice, tomato juice, ketchup, and ice cubes at a high speed. Season with salt and pepper and pour into 4 glasses. Thread 1 cherry tomato and 1 orange wedge onto each cocktail skewer and use to garnish glasses.

Red Child's Surprise

Makes 2 tall glasses
1 lb watermelon flesh, Juice of 1 lime,
Brown sugar as desired, Ice cubes as needed

Remove seeds from watermelon and chop. In a blender, combine watermelon, lime juice, sugar and about 5 ice cubes, and purée finely. Pour into champagne saucers and serve with ice cream spoons.

🍋 In the summer, serve this well-chilled melon purée over ice cubes.

🍋 Adults may want to pour ice-cold sparkling wine or Prosecco over the red juice—the result is wonderfully refreshing.

LIST OF RECIPES

Soups and Appetizers

Salads

International Entrées

Dips and Sauces

Desserts, Cakes, and Pastries

Marmalades, Jellies, and Chutneys

Beverages